Handbook for Developing Public Confidence in Schools

by
William W. Wayson
Charles Achilles
Gay Su Pinnell
M. Nan Lintz
Lila N. Carol
Luvern Cunningham
and the
Phi Delta Kappa Commission
for Developing Public Confidence in Schools

Phi Delta Kappa Educational Foundation
Bloomington, Indiana

Cover design by Char Shreve Dapena

Library of Congress Catalog Card Number 88-61690
ISBN 0-87367-798-6
Copyright © 1988 by the Phi Delta Kappa Educational Foundation
Printed in the United States of America

Phi Delta Kappa Commission for Developing Public Confidence in Schools

William W. Wayson,
   Chairperson
Ohio State University

Charles M. Achilles
University of North Carolina
   at Greensboro

John Bates
Kingston Public Schools
Kingston, Ontario, Canada

Lila N. Carol
Ohio State University

Luvern L. Cunningham
Ohio State University

Jack R. Frymier
Phi Delta Kappa International
Bloomington, Indiana

James A. Knight, Jr.
Ohio State University

Charles Mitchell
Newark Public Schools
Newark, New Jersey

Gay Su Pinnell
Ohio State University

Joseph Rogus
University of Dayton

Lonnie H. Wagstaff
University of Cincinnati

Derek L. Burleson,
   Editorial Liaison
Phi Delta Kappa International
Bloomington, Indiana

Acknowledgments

A project like this could not have been completed without the great devotion and extraordinary contributions of many people and organizations.

Karen Kerr, Joanne Littel, and Alice Ray provided their usual excellent organizational and clerical skills and held the project materials together through several rounds of data processing and several changes in the physical circumstances in which the project took place.

The candidates for school administration certification at Ohio State University in 1984 and 1985 added significantly to the analysis and interpretation of the data, while learning what good schools can be. Their penetrating questions helped to sharpen the observations we have made. Some members of those classes helped immensely in coding and evaluating data from the questionnaires. Charles and Janice Stack, in particular, devoted hours to the data "just because they liked it." Jock and Carolyn Harris and James Sements coded seemingly endless responses from the questionnaires.

David Landis somehow managed to keep the data together and organized through several office moves, while simultaneously collecting data for another project. Gay Su Pinnell assembled the quotations used in Chapter Five and prepared the first draft and several revisions of the checklists in Chapter Nine.

Although all the Commission members contributed greatly to formulating the design of the project and directing the data collection, Lila N. Carol deserves special commendation for her energy, good humor, and intelligent analyses during the initial coding sessions.

The Commission owes a special debt to Charles M. Achilles and Nan Lintz, whose skill and energy sustained the project through many months of work. In so many ways this volume is a testament to Nan Lintz's persistence and careful research skills; she did more of the tedious work and more of the conceptual groundwork for the project than any other member of the Commission or its staff.

The entire Phi Delta Kappa organization, including many local chapter members and officers, helped whenever needed. In particular, the Ohio State University Chapter has supported the project from its inception. The Phi Delta Kappa Board of Directors initiated the project and allocated the funds needed for data collection and the Commission's planning sessions. Executive Director Lowell C. Rose saw the need for the project and secured organizational resources for the Commission. Derek L. Burleson, editor of Special Publications, was an able liaison to the Commission. He and his associate editor, David Ruetschlin, provided the editorial expertise that added significantly to the quality of the volume.

Donald Anderson, dean of the College of Education, and Charles Galloway, chairperson of the Department of Educational Policy and Leadership at Ohio State University, provided encouragement as well as space and equipment needed to conduct a project of this scope. Members of Ohio State's Faculty of Educational Administration also lent moral support and provided an academic home for the project.

Finally, several hundred school personnel took time from their very busy schedules to fill out the questionnaires, which were the source of the data reported in this volume. In fact, it is they who made the book possible. But more important, they have created the kinds of schools for children and youth that make us confident about the future of education in this nation.

To all of those we are grateful.

Phi Delta Kappa Commission for
Developing Public Confidence in Schools

Preface

America in the 1980s is insecure about its world leadership. This insecurity is manifested in the widespread criticism of all public institutions, but few have been subjected to such scrutiny and demand for change as have the public schools. Three decades of social instability and institutional incertitude have fueled a lack of confidence in the schools. Moreover, educators often have been too mired in their own crisis of self-confidence to address new problems with the surety that would assuage the public's confidence. The result has been a crisis in confidence in our schools and in their capability of meeting the demands of the new Information Age.

The Phi Delta Kappa Commission for Developing Public Confidence in Schools set out to find exemplars of schools with high public confidence. We found them and we celebrate them here. Those we visited and the many others we read about certainly have restored our confidence. These schools first and foremost are *educational* institutions — and proud of it. Every child deserves schools like these. The future of our society depends on them.

We know of no better way to inspire educators and citizens to foster public confidence than by publicizing the professional services and community relationships described in these pages. We offer neither prescriptions nor panaceas; but taken as a whole, what these schools are doing provides direction to any school or school system seriously committed to improving public confidence in the schools of this nation.

William W. Wayson
for the Phi Delta Kappa Commission for
Developing Public Confidence in Schools
1 July 1988

Table of Contents

Chapter One
The Commission's Plan for Studying Public Confidence in the Schools

By the 1980s educators were acknowledging the erosion of public confidence in the schools. For example, *The School Administrator* initiated a column by Gary Marx called "Public Confidence." A survey conducted by the American Association of School Administrators on problem areas for school administrators listed public confidence as 4th out of 71 concerns in both 1980-81 and 1982-83 (AASA 1983). Other observers reported declining public confidence in schools. Cuban spoke of an "underconfident public" and the "erosion of public confidence in schooling" (Cuban 1983).

Declining confidence in education seemed to be part of a general decline in confidence in all social institutions (Lipset and Schneider 1983; Levine and Haselkorn 1984). The Harris Poll in 1981 showed that most institutions had lost public confidence between 1966 and 1981. Americans reporting a "great deal" of confidence in the medical profession had declined from 73% to 37%; in organized religion from 41% to 22%; in the military from 62% to 28%; in major businesses from 55% to 16%; in the news media from 29% to 16%; and in advertising from 21% to zero. The average percent voicing a "great deal" of confidence had fallen from 45% to 23% for all social and governmental institutions listed in the survey.

Weiler (1982) studied the connections between public confidence in education and trust in public authority. He reported that concerns over education were severe in five Western nations and shared first place with crime control in the United States. He commented:

> [T]he decline of public confidence in education is but a reflection of a much more encompassing and pervasive erosion of confidence in public authority and public institutions. This general erosion seems to have affected negatively the public's attitudes toward specific institutions, such as schools, that are sponsored and sustained by public authority. (p. 9)

As educators recognized the need to improve public confidence in the schools, Phi Delta Kappa, as well as other organizations, began to undertake efforts to address the issues related to declining public confidence. In 1982 Phi Delta Kappa issued a call for proposals for a commission to study the problem and to provide recommendations for improving public confidence in the schools.

In preparing a proposal, we assumed (in retrospect, naively) that we could extrapolate data directly from that we had collected on 500 schools with exemplary discipline for the Phi Delta Kappa Commission on Discipline (1982). Since these schools had reported exceptionally strong community relationships, it seemed reasonable to assume the data we had might well serve as a basis for a commission report on improving public confidence. Therefore, we prepared a commission proposal with the following objectives:

1. Identify school districts or individual schools that by reputation have earned high public confidence.
2. Describe the strategies and models used in these schools that have proven to be successful for achieving and maintaining public confidence.
3. Produce a handbook including strategies and/or models for helping other districts and schools improve public confidence in their schools.

As the commission members met during 1983 and 1984, it became clear that the data from schools identified earlier by the Phi Delta Kappa Commission on Discipline were an inadequate base for what we now knew had to be done. Therefore, the commission decided to identify a national sample of schools and districts that have earned high levels of public confidence in their communities.

2

Identifying Schools with Public Confidence

In addition to the list of schools having strong community support identified in the study by the Phi Delta Kappa Commission on Discipline, we used a variety of procedures to identify another group of schools. First, commission members contributed names and addresses from their network of professional contacts, and those persons were asked to nominate schools and districts that they knew to have high levels of public confidence. Second, we advertised in the newsletters of five major professional associations, asking their readers to identify schools that had high levels of public confidence. They included the Association for Supervision and Curriculum Development, the American Association of School Administrators, the National Association of Secondary School Principals, the National Association of Elementary School Principals, and Phi Delta Kappa.

We also invited the schools identified in Kappa Delta Pi's Good Schools Study (Frymier et al. 1984), which had been carefully studied from a variety of perspectives, and the schools identified in 1983 by the U.S. Department of Education's School Recognition Program initiated by then Secretary of Education Terrel Bell. Using these procedures, we identified more than 300 schools and 80 school districts that agreed to participate in our study.

Validating the Nominations

In an effort to validate whether the nominated schools and districts did enjoy sufficient public confidence to be considered exemplars, we used four techniques: 1) nominations were solicited from knowledgeable educators who could be considered expert observers; 2) we asked independent observers from the local Phi Delta Kappa chapter to observe in the school or to draw on their direct knowledge of the school to comment about the nomination; 3) we asked knowledgeable community leaders to comment about the level and sources of confidence enjoyed by the school or district; and 4) respondents from the school or district were asked to submit evidence that they enjoyed high levels of public confidence.

Many members of local Phi Delta Kappa chapters visited nominated schools in their area or gathered informed opinions from members who knew the schools and districts. They gave us reasons why a nominated school should not be included in the sample or sent us evidence that the school or district enjoyed sufficient public confidence to be included. Their generous assistance helped greatly to

3

improve the validity of the sample. Although the local community leaders did not respond in large numbers, the ones who did contributed much that was useful for validating or for clarifying the information we received from the schools and districts. An analysis of the information they provided is given in Chapter Five.

The Sample

Through the nomination and validation process, we ended with a sample of 298 public and private schools and 77 school districts that truly seemed to have high levels of public confidence. To this sample we sent a questionnaire designed to get information about any parts of their programs that might be related to public confidence. We received useful information from 240 schools and 65 districts. The Appendix contains a list of the schools and districts in the sample, plus a few others obtained from an intensive review of the literature. We added these few because their descriptions in the literature indicated they enjoyed strong public confidence in their communities. However, none of them is included in the statistical tabulations presented in this study, though sometimes we include quotations from the articles in which they are described in order to make a point.

The returns were subjected to intensive review, and from the data emerged a set of categories or themes that served as guidelines for strengthening public confidence. The results are reported in Chapters Seven and Eight.

Some Serendipitous Findings

While conducting this study, the commission gathered several other kinds of data, some of which proved to be more interesting and enlightening than the major focus of the study. For example, one of the informal sources of data that commission members collected was from "person on the street" interviews. In these brief interviews, we attempted to get a "feel" for what factors the public would report as contributing to increased confidence or loss of confidence in their schools. The commission members went into the streets, knocked on doors, stopped people in shopping malls, and talked with people they met on their travels. For each interview there was a card with two questions on it: "What causes you to gain confidence in schools?" and "What causes you to lose confidence in schools?" When the subject was not sure what was meant by "confidence," the questions were

4

rephrased: "What causes you to think a school is doing a good job?" and "What causes you to think a school is not doing a good job?"

The answers recorded on the cards became a rich source of data for subsequent commission meetings. They provided much insight into what it takes to win and lose public confidence. Chapter Five reports what we learned from the "person on the street" interviews.

Another source of data, also reported in Chapter Five, came from the community leaders who served as one form of validation for the nominated schools. We asked the respondent for each of the nominated schools to name people in the community who could tell us about their schools. We specified that these people should represent various segments of the community, such as a newspaper editor, a minister, a civil rights leader, or a politician. When the names were sent to us, we sent them a questionnaire requesting information about their school or district and about factors contributing to their having confidence or lack of confidence. Although responses were fewer than we had desired, 153 school returns and 54 district returns were usable for the preliminary analysis of factors that build public confidence in schools. These responses added considerably to what we learned from other sources of data.

The Chapters that Follow

Chapter Two discusses the crisis of confidence in our schools. It presents evidence from several sources confirming the loss of public confidence.

Chapter Three contains a definition of "confidence" that guided the work of the commission. The attention given to defining the term is intended to be more than just a researcher's academic exercise. By sharing the dilemmas we faced in defining the term, we can help readers see why we designed our study the way we did and allow them to critique our methodology and our findings.

Chapter Four is a summary of the basic approaches to winning public confidence as advocated by several schools of thought, ranging from an agricultural approach that has been successful in winning legislative and local constituent support, to advocacy approaches that make educators more uncomfortable than they should, to political and social work approaches that require educators to expand their concepts of education and their roles as educators. The summaries give examples, the advantages and disadvantages of each approach, and sources for further information.

Chapter Five discusses those factors that cause the public, or some portions of the public, to gain or to lose confidence in the schools. The data reported here stimulate exciting prospects for building new coalitions with the public to increase confidence in the schools.

Chapter Six provides an analysis of the data supplied by the schools and districts to support their claim, or their reputation, for enjoying high public confidence. At the same time, it reveals what school personnel view as proof of public confidence.

In Chapter Seven we discuss the most frequently cited characteristics of schools that enjoy public confidence. These characteristics suggest many practical ideas for practitioners and policy makers, as well as those who will educate future teachers and administrators.

Chapter Eight confirms that schools with strong public confidence have an atmosphere and an interpersonal climate that are associated with what is known about good schools in general. Consequently, efforts to build greater public confidence may yield other positive outcomes, such as improved student achievement, fewer discipline problems, and better staff morale. The discussion contains many examples taken directly from written and oral testimony given by educators whose schools enjoy all those outcomes. This chapter also describes in more detail some teachers and some schools that have little public confidence and some that have great public confidence. We report findings from other research to add descriptive data and supplemental generalizations for the reader's use.

Chapter Nine contains checklists that schools or districts can use to gather data to guide or stimulate action to improve public confidence. It also contains a description of a process that a school staff can use in identifying what activities it wishes to undertake to improve public confidence.

The references can clarify and add to what has been said in these pages. The Appendix contains a list of the schools and districts that participated in our study. By contacting them, one can undoubtedly learn about other activities that support the various recommendations made here.

Chapter Two
The Crisis of Public Confidence in the Schools

The problem we address in this volume, simply stated, is how American educators can restore public confidence in our schools. Support for the public schools in America is at a low ebb. State support has grown slightly in recent years but has not made up for earlier losses incurred by a declining economy, taxpayer revolts, and cutbacks in federal programs. Federal government officials are pressuring both Congress and some of the more vulnerable state legislatures to create incentives in the form of tuition tax credits or voucher plans, both of which threaten to erode attendance in, and support for, public schools.

A flood of reports since 1983 have criticized schools — and more recently colleges — for all manner of shortcomings. Those criticisms have eroded confidence in many schools. In another study, we found that 45% of the administrators in schools with reputations for excellence and 70% of samples of teachers and administrators from Nebraska and Texas did not feel that public confidence had been improved by the reform reports (Wayson et al. 1988, p.143). Educators in many communities have objected because the weaknesses noted in the reform reports do not apply to their school districts; yet the public assumes they do. Extensive media coverage of the reform reports, whether intentional or not, has tended to undermine confidence in public education.

Demographic and economic trends show that the public confidence crisis likely will intensify. Schools will have a larger proportion of poor, minority, and latchkey children and more children from single-parent families than ever before. These are the children that the schools have been least able to educate in the past (Hodgkinson 1985, 1988; Lewis 1985*a*, 1986*a* and *b*). At the same time, the American economy, which in the past was able to absorb dropouts or undereducated high school graduates, now is in need of a better-educated workforce with advanced technical skills. Even the more constructive reform reports, such as *A Nation Prepared: Teachers for the 21st Century* (Carnegie Forum on Education and the Economy 1986), express doubts as to whether schools can meet the challenge; and they leave open the option for other institutions to fill the need:

> There is a growing awareness that further progress is unlikely without fundamental changes in structure. In fact, we suspect that dramatic change may be easier to achieve than incremental change, given the growing frustration with political gridlock and the increasing awareness that the biggest impediment to progress is the nature of the system itself. (p. 16)

Governors and other leaders leave no doubt that the present structure of our public school system will have to change dramatically if it is to meet future needs (National Governors' Association 1986).

These are old refrains; yet they may not be sufficient to arouse a lethargic system to respond. Some of the criticism from the reform reports is exaggerated and the recommendations simplistic or unrealistic. But the need for reform is strong, and the pressure for change is persistent and supported in high places. At the same time, educators are more vulnerable than ever, because they are divided internally and are suffering a crisis of self-confidence.

The system also has lost some of its allies. The historic coalition that united labor, middle-class parents, church groups, liberals, and government agencies in support of public education has fallen into disarray. The strongest supporters of education traditionally have been those with children in school; but no more than 25% of taxpayers now have children in school (NSPRA 1983). Without this once-solid front of support, America's public schools may well be destined to become pauper schools serving only the working class and welfare families.

Other signs of declining confidence are the failure to pass school levies in many communities and middle-class flight from urban areas to suburban or private schools. To compound the problem, as education has become more "professionalized," it has become more isolated from the community. The need to re-establish links between school and community is an obvious step toward developing public confidence. Many schools need help in designing programs and practices that foster good community relationships.

What Opinion Polls Tell Us About Loss of Public Confidence

Public confidence in the schools was at an apex in the 1950s despite accusations that Johnny could not read and that administrators were building palaces. It began to decline about the time the Soviet Union launched Sputnik in 1957 and continued to decline into the 1970s.

One measure of public confidence can be found in the Gallup Poll of Public Attitudes Toward Education, published annually in the *Phi Delta Kappan* since 1969. A recurring question in the Gallup Polls since 1974 asks respondents to give their schools a "grade" of A, B, C, D, or F. In 1986 schools were given high marks (A or B) by 41%, compared to 48% who gave those grades in 1974. Those assigning Ds and Fs increased from 11% in 1974 to 16% in 1986. Despite some ups and downs over the years, these figures do indicate a gradual decline in public confidence. Although respondents with children in school tend to grade their schools higher than those without children in school, the proportion of such respondents has declined to less than one-fourth of the voting public.

Public opinion polls can serve as an indicator of public attitudes toward education, but they cannot tell us the reasons underlying the attitudes. Also, public opinion, as expressed in polls, can be strongly influenced by media attention to events that are not truly representative of what is actually going on in the schools. For example, the Gallup Poll in 1983 reported 31% grading the schools as A or B, and 20% grading them D or F. One year later in 1984, 42% graded the schools as A or B, and 15% graded them as D or F.

No doubt media coverage of education, more than fundamental improvements, had something to do with this much change in a one-year period. 1983 was the year when the reform reports started coming out, beginning with *A Nation at Risk*. It was the time when a popular president was beginning to campaign for the 1984 election on a platform of improved education, including the identification of excellent schools under the Department of Education's School Recognition Program (Bell 1988). It was also the time when both professional journals and the mass media were giving much coverage to the effective schools movement. With education receiving so much media attention, it is understandable that the public might give the schools better grades in 1984.

But educators, who give so many grades, know how inadequately grades communicate real substance; so we should be cautious about accepting opinon polls as a reliable gauge of deeply rooted public support. The number giving schools a grade of A has remained close to 10% for the past ten years, and is much less than the 18% giving an A in 1974. Few people would feel confident if they were going into an operating room where the chances of having a surgeon rated A were only one in ten.

Other Grounds for Loss of Public Confidence

Some educators may view discussions of public confidence as so much academic quibbling. They are not having any trouble in their schools at the moment, so why worry about it? Such sentiments ignore the fact that *confidence affects action*. Confidence, or lack of it, leads to actions that have consequences for every person in the school system and every citizen in the community. Some of the consequences are evident in the choices people are making about schools.

Public schools are facing greater competition for resources and enrollments than ever before. In the last two decades we have seen aggressive competition in the form of Christian schools, home schooling, magnet schools, and other alternative types of schools. Some experiments with voucher systems in the late 1960s were shortlived, but the idea persists with strong support from President Reagan and Secretary of Education William Bennett under the slogan, "give parents a choice."

A major study on alternative education choices by Bridge and Blackman (1978) concluded that the following factors are influential in parents' decisions about choosing a school:

1. Parents' childrearing values may affect their choices. Their own education and work experience has taught them that certain things are necessary for "success." They look for those things in rearing their children and in choosing a school.
2. Geographic proximity is an important factor in choosing a school, particularly among poorer parents. However, as these parents' children become teenagers and as the parents learn

more about the choices available, proximity becomes less important. When alternatives are available within a school, these parents make educationally relevant choices.

3. Better-educated parents use more sources of information in making choices about schools. They make more use of school publications and direct talks with teachers than do other parents.

4. About one-third of parents choose a school because of what is taught and how it is taught. However, curriculum factors are not of major importance in selecting a school.

5. About one-fifth of parents choose a school because of the school staff. After the choice is made, a good relationship with staff is the most important factor contributing to continuing satisfaction.

6. When lower-class parents choose an alternative school, they tend to select those with highly structured programs that stress basic skills and strict discipline. More affluent and better-educated parents tend to choose more flexible programs that stress social relationships, independent learning, and creativity.

Although parents who have no options take their public schools for granted, some parents use the quality of the schools as a primary criterion when buying or renting a house. Included in this group are affluent parents and also poorer parents who are willing to make great sacrifices to get their children in a preferred school.

Criteria used in making choices about school include the the general pedagogical approach, unique course offerings, quality of teaching staff, nature of the student body, and general atmosphere of the school (Kyle and Allen 1982). Other studies show that parents choose private schools because they are dissatisfied with, or cannot find what they want in, public schools (Williams, Hancher, and Hutner 1983). Oakley (1985) studied choices made in an affluent suburb, where parents had several private schools as well as one alternative program within the public system from which to choose. His findings confirm earlier studies, which show that direct contact with school personnel and testimony from students, neighbors, and acquaintances influence the choices parents make.

Boyer and Savageau (1985), in their rating of cities for quality of life, used the following measures for rating the quality of schools: pupil/teacher ratios, educational options at colleges and universities, and the percentage of tax revenues allocated for public schools. The authors conclude:

If there is one area of public service in which shoddy performance pushes families to change their address, it is the kind of education their children are getting in public schools.

Stickney (1986) gives this advice to prospective home-buyers:

> For families choosing a home, the buy-or-good-bye factor is often the quality of public schools in the neighborhood. . . . Whether or not you have school-age children, school quality, or lack thereof, should be an important factor in your home-buying decision since it can powerfully affect the price — and future resale value — of your home.

Stickney recommends that prospective home-buyers talk to parents in the neighborhood, to PTA officers, and to faculty of nearby teachers' colleges for information about school quality. He also points out some things to look for when visiting a school:

> If many classrooms have more [than the national average class size], that can mean children aren't getting enough individual attention. Observe what happens between classes. If the atmosphere is disconcertingly like [the movie] *Fast Times at Ridgemont High*, you may prefer another district. Do the school's facilities such as the gym or science labs look amply equipped and well used?
>
> In classes are teachers just going through the motions — or stirring up their students? Are questions asked that require only one-word answers, or must students think and explain? Is there dialogue? If arms are waving and there's a lot of energetic give-and-take, it may indeed be the kind of school where your kids should go.

Answers to the above questions will determine the level of confidence parents will have in a school. Confidence influences decisions and impels action. Sociological and political factors influencing education in the 1980s require that educators become more knowledgeable about how to secure and maintain public confidence in our schools. But not all schools are suffering a loss of public confidence. There are many schools that enjoy strong community support manifested in adequate funding, parent volunteer programs, and loyalty of students and staff. In these communities, citizens are proud of their public schools and real estate agents make the schools a major selling point to newcomers. We undertook this study to find out what factors contribute to public confidence in such schools and prepared this *Handbook* to share what we learned.

12

Chapter Three
Defining Public Confidence

One of the early tasks of the commission was to define "public confidence." It is a little like the planet Pluto; astronomers knew it was there for years before they ever saw it on a telescope because they could observe its gravitational effect on other parts of the solar system. But they had a hard time finding what they knew had to be there. Public confidence is not something that is easy to see or measure, but we know it is there. And we know that it disposes people toward actions that directly affect both communities and school personnel. The commission concluded that it was a concept worthy of study and after considerable deliberation adopted the following working definition:

> *Confidence is belief in, faith in, pride in, loyalty to, understanding of, and willingness to support and defend a school or school system.*

Another problem in defining "public confidence" is that there is not one public, but many whose expectations sometimes conflict with one another. Yet many studies show that persons with widely different views nevertheless share basic values about the outcomes of schooling. Our findings show much commonality among the different publics as to what factors they feel contribute to confidence in

13

schools. However, school personnel who want to gain public confidence must be aware that their community is a loose conglomeration of publics, each of which reacts to different features of the school. As we shall see, most schools that gain confidence from their publics value diversity and strive to meet many needs and interests.

The Invalidity of Popular Measures

Anyone trying to assess public confidence must be aware of the lack of validity of many of the popular measures of school quality used as indicators of confidence. To illustrate this point, consider this excerpt from a letter sent to a publication that had carried an article that rated schools in central Ohio.

> Our primary concern with the ratings is that they were based predominantly on financial criteria . . . per-pupil expenditures; teacher-student ratios; teacher experience; "discussions" with state department and local school personnel. Three of these focus solely upon the financial ability of a district. We feel strongly that one simply can't equate dollars spent to the quality of a school district. . . . [T]he following information substantiates our contention that the Pickerington schools merited a better rating than the tie for 12th. (McClurg, Ross, and Ball 1987)

The writers go on to list the many accomplishments of their school district: more National Merit Semifinalists than nine of the 11 schools rated more highly; ACT composite scores higher than eight of the schools rated more highly; a middle-school science Olympiad team finishing second in the state and 15th nationally; higher academic requirements for eligibility in extracurricular activities than required by the state; all three elementary schools (more than any other district) cited as Hall of Fame schools by the Ohio Association of Elementary School Principals; a nationally recognized marching band that performed at three NFL games as well as the Gimbels Thanksgiving Day Parade; a thorough study of its special education programs resulting in more programs to serve students with special needs; 17 league championships in various sports in the past five years and the girls' state champion basketball team in 1985; no use of temporary or portable buildings despite significant population growth; and passage of a 9.8 mill operating levy. After recounting these accomplishments, the writers continue:

> Pickerington does not have the tax base of other districts, nor do we spend as much per student as the majority of districts

14

rated above us. We do, however, pride ourselves on the quality education that we provide in spite of the lesser amount of money we have available. . . . We firmly believe you need to look beyond simply the financial information and look more closely at indicators of a quality instructional program.

The letter's point is well-founded; and it highlights the difficulties that school personnel, the media, and the public itself have in rating schools. The accomplishments listed above to support a higher rating are impressive, and they may truly reflect the efforts of a dedicated staff and a supportive community. On the other hand, in some school systems such accomplishments may reflect priorities given to a few students or a few activities. No amount of touting these accomplishments is going to garner confidence from parents whose children are not well served by a championship basketball team or a first-class marching band.

Many factors commonly used to assess school quality do not necessarily indicate public confidence. Accrediting teams often count volumes in the library or measure space allocations, but the public may not even know about those factors. A district with a large tax base may spend funds in ways that impress the public, but a high per-pupil expenditure does not necessarily account for public confidence. The percentage of graduates from high-income families enrolling in college, however high, may be lower than the public expects; thus it may not be a valid measure of public confidence. There are many risks in using such factors to identify schools with high public confidence.

We did not use such factors to identify the schools and districts that participated in our study. Rather, we asked various publics what schools had high public confidence. Then we tried to assess what factors those publics used in making their judgments. We have tried to report accurately what school personnel and others in the community said were the factors in their schools that contributed to confidence.

The Accumulation of Acclaim

We have used a reputational approach to identify the schools in our study. Many of them have received ratings of excellence or have won competitive awards, which can be considered as measures of quality. Using such schools to study public confidence has its limitations. Winning an award gives a school visibility and increases its chances of winning other awards; it also reduces the chances that other schools will be recognized. The measures of quality that cause a school to win the initial award tend to be the same ones that cause it to be recognized for subsequent awards. Of the schools we surveyed, many staff and students had received a number of awards and commendations. One of the schools from our sample reports:

> *Money Magazine* (September 1981) listed us as one of 12 best schools. In 1983, we received the U.S. Department of Education's Excellence in Education Recognition, and *Parade Magazine* (1 January 1984) listed us as one of 15 best public schools. We have a nationally recognized Advanced Placement program and have been chosen as the leading feeder to the University of California at Berkeley and to San Francisco State University, and second feeder to the University of California at Davis.
> — Lowell High School, San Francisco, California

One award leads to another. Once a school starts receiving awards and recognitions, it is more likely to be nominated for other awards. This seems to have been the case for many of the schools in our sample. Consequently, some deserving but as yet unrecognized schools may not be included.

Rational and Emotional Factors Influencing Public Confidence

Public confidence is based on both rational and emotional factors. Consideration must be given to both. The rational approach to building confidence in the schools is to give the public the facts that show why a school is good. But emotional factors may cause a person to believe that a school is the best (or the worst) in the world despite facts showing that it is not. When emotional factors cause the public to lose faith and trust in the schools, restoring confidence is difficult no matter what the facts are. Negative attitudes tend to persist; and even when facts are available, they are used selectively to maintain negative attitudes.

While recognizing the emotional factors involved in gaining or losing confidence, the commission decided that public confidence is linked to tangible actions that can be described and serve as guides for others. This *Handbook* includes descriptions of specific actions schools have taken to develop public confidence in their communities, but the emotional elements of confidence are evident throughout, particularly where we discuss the "caring" school (Chapter Seven) and the factors that cause the public to lose confidence (Chapter Eight).

Traditional Rational Approaches to Public Confidence

School-community relations is the term traditionally used to describe a rational approach to fostering public confidence in the schools. Typically, a central office staff person is assigned responsibility for school-community relations. Approaches used tend to be rational and cognitive with facts flowing (usually only one way) to the community. The turnout for spectator events or parent-teacher meetings is seen as an indication of confidence. Efforts to stimulate community involvement, such as open house for parents once a year, are limited and controlled. Newsletters from the central office communicate official business and showcase outstanding programs, but the communication is mostly one way.

Another approach to school-community relations is the use of local opinion polls. Such polls are viewed as one measure of public confidence or lack thereof, but polls can distort if the questions asked are stated in such a way that they elicit only positive responses or if the sample represents only the power group in the community. Sometimes poll results can give school officials a false sense of confidence, because the polls blind them to the concerns of subgroups in the community.

Although the rational and cognitive approaches used in traditional school-community relations are helpful, they do not provide the personal interaction and participation that engender the kind of loyalty and commitment needed for true public confidence. Confidence results from a blend of positive feelings and accurate information about a school. Traditionally, school officials have done a better job of providing the public with accurate information than they have with developing positive feelings. A parent who walks into a school and sees a large sign with the message, "All visitors must report to the principal's office," is not likely to have positive feelings about the school. Teachers who restrict their contact with parents only to scheduled parent-teacher conferences and the annual "Open House" are not seen by parents as friendly advocates for their children. Many of the schools in this study seemed to know how to blend positive feelings and accurate information to foster public confidence in their communities. Quite simply, they market their schools better.

17

Confidence as a "Flow of Images"

Another way of understanding public confidence is the "flow of images" concept (Lasswell 1971; Carol and Cunningham 1984). These are the multiple impressions that combine in people's minds to make them feel confident about a school or school system or about some particular individual in the system. Sometimes the flow of images is fleeting and subconscious; other times the images are intense and thoroughly examined. Employers' flow of images may focus on what local high school graduates are able or unable to do in the workplace. Mothers' flow of images may focus on what their children told them went on in school today. Those mothers, in turn, talk to their neighbors or to a person in the checkout line at the supermarket, and the responses they receive become part of the continuing flow of images. Parents may form strong convictions based on the brief flow of images arising from attending the school's annual "Open House," though it is unlikely. This view holds that confidence may flow from images formed over time by events widely separated in time and place (Cunningham 1981).

Recognizing how a flow of images influences public confidence, educators can exert some influence over what images are projected in the community. Even though the public filters images through emotional lenses, if educators do all they can to keep the flow of images positive, then they can "bank" confidence, which can be drawn on when crises occur.

How Do School Officials Determine Whether They Have Public Confidence?

From the schools participating in this study, we wanted to determine what they considered as tangible evidence of public confidence from their constituents. In the questionnaire we asked: "Think about evidence that shows that your school has earned a high degree of public confidence, then check any of the following list of indicators that are generally true for your school." Table 3.01 contains the list of indicators and the percent of responses. These indicators could be used by other schools for assessing the level of public confidence.

All of the indicators in Table 3.01 were reported by more than half of the schools, which is not surprising since these schools were selected for having high levels of public confidence. The greatest number reported parent involvement and interest beyond the spectator level. Positive publicity for student and staff achievement also

Table 3.01
Indicators of Public Confidence Reported by Schools

Indicator	*Percent*
1. A high level of parent involvement and interest beyond being spectators at school events.	92
2. Parents who have other choices choose to enroll their children in this school.	89
3. Positive publicity/reporting on the school by the media.	87
4. Many awards have been given to students or to the school for academic achievement, community/social service, etc.	81
5. A high level of community involvement and interest beyond being spectators at school events.	79
6. Verbal or written expressions of confidence addressed to the school board, school officials, or to the media.	77
7. Exceptional community support for sports programs or other extracurricular activities.	69
8. A history of levies passed or other financial support for the school or district.	67
9. Exceptional numbers of parents or community/business persons volunteer in the school.	62
10. Exceptionally high attendance at parent-teacher meetings and conferences.	58

received high marks as an indicator of confidence. Passing levies, exceptional attendance at extracurricular activities and parent meetings or conferences, and community volunteers in the school all were seen as indicators that the community values what the schools are doing.

Respondents also were asked to list any additional evidence of confidence not inclued in the list of indicators. Some of their contributions, which seem to be valid evidence of public support and confidence, were:

"Students from out of town enrolled in our school."
"New residents tend to locate in our school area."
"We have a waiting list to enter our school."
"Our district is growing while others around us are declining."
"Real estate people use the school as an important selling point."
"Other schools send delegations to observe in our school."
"We conduct parent surveys and they give us high marks and ratings."

"We have high levels of attendance and few dropouts."
"We have secured grants to support our program."
"We are a base for training teachers."

The kinds of evidence cited above can be used as measures of public confidence. They are tangible and specific actions that school officials can use to define "public confidence."

Summary

Although confidence in schools is difficult to define or measure, we know it impels and directs action that has an impact on everyone associated with the schools. It springs from both knowledge and feelings of many different publics. Personnel in high-confidence schools define confidence in terms of a variety of supportive measures they receive from their communities.

Chapter Four
Approaches to Building
Public Confidence

Much of the school-community relations literature is addressed to administrators and offers such general advice as "involve your community in your school" or "know the power structure." Little attention is given to teachers and other staff who have the most direct contact with the community and are in a position to exert the most influence in shaping the community's attitudes about the schools. What is needed is a broadened perspective of school-community relations.

In this chapter we shall look at some different approaches to building public confidence derived from fields other than education. They include agriculture, social work, public relations, and marketing, among others. None of these approaches is distinct unto itself; each borrows from the others. But taken together, they provide educators with a broader repertoire for building strong school-community relations.

Agricultural Approach

This approach uses the strategies of the agricultural extension agent, who works with adults and students in both formal and informal settings, often under the guidance of an advisory council. This approach has a long tradition dating back to the Smith-Hughes Act of 1917. Through such organizations as the Future Farmers of America and the 4-H, the teacher or extension agent establishes close ties with

21

students and their families, making home visits and assisting students with their projects.

The community-service orientation of the agricultural approach helps to build a strong constituency. Through on-site visits, a teacher develops a close working relationship with students and their families, receives direct feedback from them, and wins their confidence and respect. This approach to building public confidence demands a wider range of skills for teachers than those typically used in the classroom. And it requires time commitments beyond the normal school day. Although this approach grew out of an agricultural tradition that today serves only a small proportion of the student population, it deserves careful consideration as a model for school-community relations.

Marketing Approach

This approach uses marketing techniques from the business world with the goal of "selling" educational programs and services specifically geared to various segments of the community. The techniques used include interactive communication and needs assessment, which provide feedback from the community through questionnaires or broad-based advisory committees and are followed up by much planning and development work by the school staff. The marketing approach allows school officials to focus their energies on specific areas identified by the needs assessment. The resulting programs and services show the public that the school system is responsive to the community's identified needs.

The marketing approach can help educators design better programs and can conserve resources. In using the marketing approach, school officials must be careful not to "oversell" and then not be able to deliver. They should also be alert to resentment arising from the use of resources that some constituencies feel should be used for other purposes. The staff may have to be convinced of the value of soliciting feedback that may be negative.

Public Relations Approach

This approach is commonly used — and sometimes misused — by school systems. It involves a variety of strategies to promote a positive image of the schools, including sending newsletters and other communications to parents, forming "booster clubs" for athletic teams and marching bands, distributing buttons or bumper stickers with

"Support Your School" messages, and sending student groups to perform for civic organizations.

All these strategies are appropriate for letting the community know about the good things going on in the school. They present the school in a positive way. However, they tend to be one-way communication and do not allow for much community feedback. They also may be covering up real problems in the school that need to be addressed.

Political Approach

This approach is used mostly by school administrators and designated central office staff in order to create constituencies in various segments of the community to support the schools. Through involvement on advisory committees or "blue ribbon" task forces, citizens become committed to improving the schools and often work to gain support from other citizens. When representation includes all segments of the community, various points of view can be expressed. Participation on citizen committees or task forces serves as a good training ground for future leaders.

Political strategies for building public confidence are consistent with a democratic society, but they can be compromised if citizen representation is restricted to an "in" group who are perceived as always "running the show," or if their role is only to "rubber stamp" the decisions of the school administration. There is also the danger that those who volunteer for citizen groups come with a hidden agenda that may not be in the best interest of the schools.

Advocacy Approach

This approach is used by outside advocacy groups to raise community awareness of the the needs and rights of children and to lobby for public support of the schools to serve those needs. Examples of the advocacy approach are the organized efforts by parents of handicapped, gifted, or minority children to secure appropriate education. Strategies include various forms of networking, public information campaigns, and lobbying legislators and school boards.

Groups involved in the advocacy approach tend to have strong organizational skills and are persistent in the pursuit of their goals. They have a sophisticated understanding of the change process and are usually effective lobbyists. Sometimes advocacy groups are threatening to the education establishment; and there is potential for conflict with school boards and teacher unions if their demands are perceived as a grab for power.

Social Work Approach

This approach uses strategies from the field of social work in such areas as community development, social planning, and social action. The school serves as a community center for education and recreation as well as a liaison with local social agencies. The school provides a base from which citizens can mobilize to deal with such community problems as drug abuse, teenage pregnancy, crime, and vandalism. Community leaders often learn the skills of organization and advocacy needed for neighborhood improvement projects.

Social work strategies for building public confidence bring educators and local citizens together to work on problems affecting both students and the community at large. The schools and social agencies become partners in serving students and their families. These strategies require teachers and administrators to move beyond their traditional instructional roles. There is also potential for conflict when proposed social action threatens the power structure of the community. Nevertheless, these strategies are powerful means for building a grassroots constituency to support schools.

Educational Program Approach

This approach includes all efforts to improve the educational program to ensure that every child is learning. As a foundation for any of the other approaches to building public confidence, this one holds the greatest potential for developing long-lasting support for the schools. Strategies used include ongoing programs of curriculum development and instructional improvement. They call for staff involvement in problem identification, needs assessment, and inservice education.

These strategies are the ones educators may be best prepared to carry out, especially if they have had training in curriculum improvement and staff development. But these are a long-term effort; results are not quickly apparent. Often marketing and public relations approaches are necessary to communicate school improvement efforts to parents and the public. But when a school staff works continuously to improve the instructional program, solid, long-lasting public confidence usually results.

Summary

The overview of approaches to building public confidence described above is intended to provide school officials with options. Each approach has its merits, but different approaches are needed for different communities and different circumstances. Some approaches require a greater investment of time and effort than others, but they are likely to have the most enduring effects. We found examples of all the approaches being used in the schools and districts with high public confidence.

Chapter Five
What Does the Public Want?
Factors Influencing
Confidence in Schools

One way to assess public confidence is to look at schools that already have it and then see what those schools are doing. That is what the commission originally set out to do, and we report what we found in Chapters Six and Seven. Another way is to ask the public directly what causes them to gain or lose confidence in schools. That is what we report in this chapter.

Early in the study, the commission decided to get a sampling of opinions about what factors caused people to have confidence in the schools and what factors caused them to lose confidence. Each commission member agreed to interview people on the streets, in places of business, in lunch rooms, and in other public sites. We make no claim for the representativeness of our sample; our purpose was simply to identify some of the factors contributing to public confidence or loss of confidence.

The first round of interviews was conducted in New Jersey, Ohio, and Tennessee, which resulted in usable data from 148 respondents. The responses were so interesting that we decided to validate them by conducting further interviews in Indiana and Illinois. From these two states, we obtained usable data from 261 respondents. The findings from the total sample of 409 were so consistent that we felt we had useful data that educators would do well to consider when assessing public confidence in their communities.

We asked our subjects two questions: "What causes you to have confidence in schools?" and "What causes you to lose confidence in schools?" The open-ended responses were analyzed to determine what common themes might emerge. The interview data were categorized by themes and ranked according to the number of times that a particular theme appeared.

Table 5.01 shows the ranking of the themes for both those factors that raise public confidence and those that result in a loss of public confidence.

Table 5.01

Ranking of 20 Categories of Responses for Gain or Loss of Confidence in Schools as Expressed by Citizens in Three Surveys

Gain			Loss	
n	Rank	Confidence Reasons	n	Rank
247	1	Teacher attitudes	223	1
153	2	Administrator attitudes	119	3
122	3	Student attitudes	74	6
120	4	Academic programs	60	9
116	5	Communications	72	7
93	6	Community attitudes	77	5
91	7	Academic performance	52	10
54	8	Instructional quality	46	11
53	9	Community involvement	22	16
48	10	Staff quality	65	8
43	11.5	Non-academic programs	23	15
43	11.5	Decision-making process	130	2
41	13	Discipline	109	4
35	14	Career/college readiness	26	14
21	15.5	Buildings/facilities	32	13
21	15.5	Funding	44	12
13	17	Materials/equipment	19	17.5
8	19	Equal opportunities	16	19
8	19	Salaries	11	20
8	19	Student/teacher ratio	19	17.5

Note: Ties are shown as equal ranks.

27

Factors Affecting Gains and Losses in Confidence

1. The highest ranking factor contributing to public confidence is the perception that teachers care for students, for learning, and for the school. How teachers act or are perceived to act appears to have a strong influence on the level of confidence people have in their schools. If teachers are brusque or rude with parents, if they complain about their work and working conditions; if they do not seem to care about students, then they are contributing mightily to the decline in public confidence in the schools.

> I got nothing out of her. I would sit there and ask a question, and it was like talking to a wall. I expected a teacher to be more alert and more attentive to what David was or was not doing. But she wasn't giving me anything.

> I get tired of talking to teachers; all they do is complain and put down their profession. And these are usually your worst teachers.

Conversely, when teachers project positive attitudes about their work and about students, they are a major force in developing public confidence in the schools.

> There are teachers who really care about their job. They are so excited about what they are teaching. These are the classes in which kids learn the most.

> She was willing to listen to me as a parent. I just had good positive feelings when Sean was there with her. There was a positive charge between them. Sean looked at her when she talked. He did not put his head down. He wasn't ashamed because she confirmed that Sean is trying. And he sensed that.

2. The factor ranking second is the perception that the principal cares about students.

> My husband and I went to the principal, and he admitted that Mrs. Cox and Carl were having a hard time. When we asked if there was a possibility that Carl could change teachers, she said absolutely not. She said she stood behind her teachers and she wouldn't do anything. She wouldn't budge. So Carl stayed in Mrs. Cox's room and did nothing and stayed in his corner.

If this sample is indicative of the broader public's attitude, then those who work most closely with children must realize what an important influence they have on public confidence. Currently the literature on school-community relations gives little attention to the key role teachers and other building-level staff can play in enhancing the school or district's reputation. Steps must be taken to make teachers aware of their important role and to prepare them to carry out that role.

3. Communications from the school to the community help raise public confidence.

> The honor rolls and school events are published in the paper. They show that our students are participating and are doing well academically compared with other area schools.

4. Communication among neighbors and others in the community has much impact on the attitudes citizens express about confidence or lack of confidence in the schools.

> I've heard some parents make very negative comments regarding the problems they have had in getting assistance for their children who have learning difficulties.

> My confidence comes when I talk to kids and hear positive things about what they are doing at school. When the children see purpose in their classes and enjoy learning, that tells me that something is being done right.

> I feel confident because I hear from students and parents alike that lessons and teaching methods are being varied.

5. The public expects schools to maintain good discipline, so good discipline in itself does not foster public confidence. However, when the public perceives that discipline is poor, there is a major loss of confidence.

> Newspaper articles that deal with youth crime in the school district turn us off, as does seeing rude, undisciplined behavior at school events or anywhere else in the community. Some teachers speak negatively of their work and the students they work with.

> Continual media attention given to the faults of education makes it hard not to believe that there are shortcomings and inequities in our schools; for example, the discipline problems and high dropout rates in large schools in the inner city.

6. Good decision-making processes do not necessarily contribute to public confidence; but when the decision-making processes used in making school policy are suspect, then a major loss of confidence occurs.

The public expects school officials to make policy decisions necessary for the orderly operation of the school system; and under normal circumstances, they pay little attention to how decisions are made. However, if some crisis arises that affects a significant number of citizens, such as the decision to close a school, then the decision-making process comes under scrutiny and confidence is likely to deteriorate.

7. Academic programs, particularly those providing a variety of opportunities for different types of learners, were seen as contributing to gains in confidence.

> The school in my home town offered a greater variety of classes, including Advanced Placement courses, whereas this school has only four years of English and the basic math and science courses. I believe the best education comes from the other school.

> I think public schools are encouraging students to enter college-prep programs. I also think that schools are helping students by adding computer classes. With this being the age of computers, it is good for kids to be exposed to them.

8. Staff quality as measured by credentials held or degrees earned did not rate high as a factor related to confidence.

Of course, communities differ in their attitudes about a school staff's professional credentials and advanced degrees; but our data suggest that they are not as important a factor in public confidence as are teachers who demonstrate that they care about students.

9. Students' successful academic performance is related somewhat with gains in confidence, but poor performance is related somewhat less with loss of confidence.

> Catering to athletes reduces my confidence in schools. I'm also upset by the unnerving reality that some high school graduates can't read or write. Basics such as these should be first priority, and no one should slip through the school system without them. Kids that can't speak or write well make me wonder how they move up a grade every year. Some of the older teens are lacking adequate communication skills, and yet they are looking at graduation in a year or two. That is surprising!

> Now, you know schools are OK when you see student motivation and interest in school and when test scores improve. Student interest in extracurricular activities also lets you know.

The relationship between student achievement and public confidence does not seem to be as strong as conventional wisdom would suggest. Interview data and observations in school support the tentative conclusion that communities establish achievement levels that are thought to be attainable by most of their students. If achievement conforms to those expectations, then confidence is maintained. Only if the community is aware that achievement or performance has increased well beyond expectations is there likely to be a significant rise in confidence.

Expected achievement or performance levels will differ among communities. One may emphasize college preparation while another may focus on championship sport teams or musical performance. These expectations reflect community traditions. When student achievement exceeds community expectations to a significant degree, then the school increases confidence and becomes a major force in raising community expectations.

10. Effective instructional methods are related somewhat with public confidence, and poor instructional practices are related somewhat less with loss of confidence.

11. Community involvement is related somewhat with gains in confidence, but lack of involvement does not seem to result in loss of confidence.

12. Extracurricular or non-academic programs seem only moderately related to gains in confidence, but poor quality extracurricular programs ranked very low as a cause for loss of confidence.

> We see classes doing community projects or going out into the public to learn. That is visible evidence of good education. We also have schools where they have rallies, plays, and musicals, which demonstrate a lot of spirit.

13. The condition of buildings and facilities were not viewed as highly related to public confidence, but poor conditions were considered a minor factor for a loss of confidence.

> I have my doubts when I pass by a school and the outside appearance and the behavior of the students looks negative.

14. Preparing students for careers or higher education was a relatively minor factor contributing to gains or losses in public confidence.

This factor no doubt differs from community to community. Although it was mentioned infrequently by respondents in our sample, it could take on greater significance in communities where the num-

31

ber of graduates who get successful jobs or attend college falls below community expectations.

15. Programs for promoting equal educational opportunities were ranked very low as causes for gains or losses in confidence (except among minority respondents).

Although our sample included a number of respondents from lower socioeconomic levels, few racial and ethnic minorities were represented. Equity issues might have been reported more frequently if our sample had included more minorities. In our view, the public, of whatever background, tends to look less at formal programs and more to the attitudes of staff who have direct contact with students when assessing the school's efforts to deal with equity issues.

Our data collection methods did not allow us to elicit sensitive information about how race or social class influences public confidence (exceptions were the occasional comment from a real estate agent or school official). It seems that confidence in schools is related to citizens' prior attitudes about race and social class. That is, those who feel that the presence of lower-class whites and minority students reduces a school's quality will not have confidence in a school that enrolls such students until they have had a positive experience in the school. Fears diminish among parents who have children in the school and are knowledgeable about its operation. Confidence in schools serving a mixed socioeconomic student body is enhanced when the staff communicates a caring attitude about children and provides assurance that quality instruction and learning are going on in the school.

Lack of confidence seems to be most prevalent just before and during the initial stages of a dramatic transition, such as desegregating a school. Anxiety and fears are intensified where there is negative publicity, political infighting, resistance from school officials, delays in implementation, and failure to communicate about how change is to be managed. When individuals or groups actively oppose the change, confidence waivers.

What Community Leaders Say Contributes to Gains and Losses in Public Confidence

In addition to the data summarized above, which was collected through interviews of "people on the streets," another source of data about public confidence in the schools is from the questionnaires returned by community leaders. The names of these community leaders were supplied by officials from schools or districts in our study, which were nominated as having high public confidence. Although our intent in contacting this group of community leaders was to have them validate the data supplied by the schools in our study, the information they provided also serves the purposes of this chapter. The data reported in Table 5.02 are from 153 community leaders who commented about specific schools and 54 who commented on school districts. The data are informative, and they tend to corroborate the generalizations from the larger sample of "people on the street" (Carol and Cunningham 1984).

Table 5.02
Ranking of Responses from Community Leaders about Sources of Confidence at School Building Level

Rank	Confidence Reasons	No. of Responses
1.5	Dedicated, committed teachers	75
1.5	Special instructional & extracurricular programs	75
3.5	Effective administrators	61
3.5	Buildings and grounds	61
5	Student-centered "caring" atmosphere	51
6	Positive attitudes of students/staff	40
7	Student discipline	38
8	Good curriculum	36
9	Student achievement	30
10	Parent participation	28
11	Communication with parents	22
12	Public image	22
13.5	High standards, goals, expectations	15
13.5	Board/superintendent relations, policies, decisions	15
15	Administrator/staff community service	13
16	Courteous office staff	12
17	Linkages with other institutions	11
18	Success of graduates	10
19.33	Student awards, honors	9
19.33	Testing, guidance, & counseling programs	9
19.33	Community involvement with school	9
22	Adequate funding	5
23	Student dress	4
24.5	Equity	3
24.5	Community education	3

Note: Ties are shown as equal ranks.

Community leaders mentioned most frequently "dedicated, committed teachers" as the primary factor contributing to their sense of confidence in the schools. "Special instructional programs and extracurricular activities" also were mentioned frequently. "Effective administrators" and "well-maintained buildings and grounds" were mentioned next. Ranking fifth was a "student-centered, caring atmosphere," just ahead of "positive attitudes of students and staff." Clearly, the high ranking given to a staff's caring for students confirms the assumption that persons closest to students are a major factor in determining public confidence.

It is noteworthy that community leaders have high regard for diversity in school programs to serve special populations, such as the handicapped or the gifted, and for special opportunities in music, art, and out-of-class experiences, such as field trips and extracurricular activities. They also valued administrators who were effective in working with teachers as a cohesive team and who solved problems brought to them by staff, students, or parents. They perceived effective principals as setting the tone for the humane, caring values that marked their schools.

These community leaders valued clean and well-maintained buildings and grounds and perceived these conditions as a reflection of the "caring" they valued so highly. Their favorable comments about discipline tended to focus on courtesy and general civility as expressed in school spirit and positive student attitudes. Some mentioned the staff's expectations for high standards of conduct and their efforts to be firm and fair in enforcing those standards.

Curriculum and student achievement were mentioned much less frequently than the factors discussed above. When they were mentioned, high standards for student learning, teaching basic skills, and examples of innovative curricula were cited as factors contributing to confidence.

Community involvement did not seem to be important for this group. When it was mentioned, it was more often in reference to having educators active in the community than having community members involved in the school.

"Testing programs or results," "counseling programs," "adequate funding," "student dress," and "equity issues" were mentioned infrequently as factors influencing public confidence. This may come as a surprise to educators, who are likely to consider them more important.

At the school district level, factors influencing public confidence mentioned most frequently were school board-superintendent relations, their decision-making processes, and their responsiveness to community concerns. Confidence in administrators tended to emanate from the actions of central office staff and building principals as they met the public or responded to issues of public concern.

Table 5.03
Ranking of Responses from Community Leaders about Sources
of Confidence at School District Level

Rank	Confidence Reasons	No. of Responses
1.5	Dedicated, competent teachers	22
1.5	Special instructional and extracurricular programs	22
3	Buildings and grounds	20
4	Board/superintendent relations, policies, decisions	19
5	Effective administrators	17
6	Public image	14
7	Good curriculum	12
8.3	High standards, goals, expectations	6
8.3	Student achievement	6
8.3	Success of graduates	6
11.3	Parent participation	4
11.3	Community education	4
11.3	Linkages with other institutions	4
14	Communication with parents	3
15.3	Equity	2
15.3	Testing, guidance, counseling programs	2
15.3	Administrator/staff community service	2
18	Student honors, awards	1

Note: Ties are shown as equal ranks.

What Factors Do Community Leaders Say Contribute to Loss of Confidence?

When these community leaders were asked what factors lead to a loss of confidence in their community's schools, most did not respond to the question or simply answered "none." This is understandable since the schools or districts where these community leaders lived had been selected because of their high level of public confidence. However, a few did cite factors or incidents that resulted in a loss of confidence.

The ones mentioned most frequently were: failure to address racial issues (including, in a few cases, giving too much attention to racial minorities); drug or alcohol abuse or rumors of such abuse; overemphasis on interscholastic athletics; the teaching of values with which the respondent disagreed or the failure to teach values that the respondent thought important; and the failure of administrators to do something about "incompetent" or "uncaring" teachers.

Where Does the Public Get Its Information?

Community leaders were asked to indicate what information sources affected their impressions about schools or districts and which of these sources were most influential. Their responses, summarized in Table 5.04, show that for both schools and districts, school employees rank first as sources of information and their information is the most influential. School children and parents of school children rank second and third, respectively, as important and influential sources of information about the schools. Clearly, the people in the schools and those directly served by them are considered the most important and most influential sources of information about schools. Their influence touches many members of the community who have no other contacts with the schools. Their word-of-mouth communication seems to have more influence than other sources of information.

Community leaders also were asked to indicate who was responsible for a recent activity that caused them to gain confidence in the schools. Their responses, summarized in Table 5.05, show that gains in confidence in individual schools were more the result of actions initiated *in* schools than by actions taken at the district level. Teachers were the most important actors, followed by the principal, other certified personnel (counselors or librarians), and noncertified personnel (secretaries, custodians, or food-service workers). At the district level, the superintendent was the most important actor, followed by personnel who work in the individual school buildings. Clearly, the most important actors for building public confidence in schools are those people who work most closely with children; and they also are highly important in building confidence for the school district.

Table 5.04
Source and Influence of Impression About Schools
Among Community Leaders*
(School N = 192; District N = 67)

	Source of Impression		Most Influential Impression	
	School	District	School	District
School employees	80%	82%	51%	44%
School children	74	75	22	21
Parents of school children	73	81	13	8
PTA	30	28	2	5
Media	23	51	1	7
School board	23	51	1	5

*Respondents could check more than one response.

Table 5.05
Who Was Responsible for Actions That Built Confidence?*
(Schools N = 192; Districts N = 67)

Person	School	District
Teachers	65%	45%
Principal	63	39
Non-classroom certified person	42	34
Non-certified school person	30	9
School community (general)	22	24
School board	15	31
Students	15	7
Superintendent	15	48
Other central office staff	11	27

*Respondents could check more than one response.

Summary

The factors identified in this chapter as contributing to gains and losses in confidence should alert educators to what they must do or avoid doing in order to foster public confidence in the schools. Public confidence stems from information and attitudes communicated both formally and informally through networks that begin with those who work in the schools. Published or broadcast information, while useful, has less impact than personal communications. Such factors as student achievement, discipline, decision-making processes, and the condition of physical facilities have less impact on public confidence than most educators suspect — unless they fall below community expectations. Teachers and principals — and to a lesser extent, superintendents and school board members — are the key persons in influencing public confidence. They also can raise a community's expectations for its schools by calling attention to student achievements, by maintaining high morale, and by communicating a caring attitude toward students.

Chapter Six
Characteristics of Schools with
High Public Confidence

If educators are asked about school-community relations, they are likely to discuss only those efforts that might best be described as public relations. Such discussions tell little about what actually is going on to influence public confidence. They yield findings akin to telling a man to wax his car while neglecting to mention the need for regular maintenance under the hood. Our study attempted to avoid superficial public relations responses by first identifying schools with high public confidence and then asking officials from these schools to describe their schools and communities. They responded by describing a rich array of practices, which seem to be major factors contributing to the public confidence they enjoy.

These high-confidence schools work hard to serve their communities, and they let the public know about their efforts. They act like winners. They are success-oriented, and they "sell" their success.

> There are four basic rules for an effective public relations program: 1) do a good job; 2) do a good job; 3) do a good job; 4) tell someone about it.
> — Shaker Heights (Ohio) School District

These schools recognize that no one single factor can create public confidence. Rather, it results from a blend of people, skills, and conditions that are unique to their school and community. They do not rely on a "public relations" office or on championship athletic teams to garner community support. Their support derives from an array of attributes and activities that in combination foster public confidence.

> I don't know that these characteristics are singularly unique; but when blended together, they produce a positive synergy from which the students benefit.
> — Albion Junior High School, Strongville, Ohio

> Not all persons in the community are aware of the curriculum and instructional program or of the academic accomplishments. But as they observe the appearance of the building, the deportment of the students, the number and quality of activities and projects executed by the school, and the cooperative and caring relationship among the staff, students, and parents, they are able to make inferences about the effectiveness of the school program. Their confidence results from a belief that the things that are readily observable have implications that are not visible on the surface.
> — Pershing Elementary School, University City, Missouri

The responses from the questionnaires submitted by these schools fall into three broad areas that contribute to the high public confidence they enjoy:

1. *Characteristics of the Setting.* Respondents described positive attributes of the setting, including staff, students, physical facilities, program, and the community. These attributes may or may not be within the control of school officials; they are the "givens" with which school officials have to work.

2. *Attitudes and Values.* Respondents described attitudes and values held by persons inside and outside the school setting, which they felt contributed to their success. These attitudes and values affect the nature of the relationships between the school and community and predispose people to take actions that elicit confidence.

3. *Activities.* Respondents described activities and programs that won public support and could be replicated in other school settings.

This chapter presents characteristics of the setting and attitudes and values most frequently reported by the schools nominated as having high public confidence. Their activities and programs are reported in Chapter Seven. The information reported here shows that these schools engage their communities in ways that produce positive outcomes in both the schools and their communities. They capitalize

40

on the potential of their communities, and as a result bring out positive changes in their settings.

Most Frequently Reported Characteristics
of Schools with High Public Confidence

*1. Respondents described students' characteristics far more fre-
quently than any other element of their school.* This attention to students reflects the staff's intuitive, if not intentional, response to the
public's desire to have schools staffed by personnel who care for students. It may also reflect the staff's tendency to judge themselves
and their schools by the qualities their students bring to school with
them. Respondents described their students as "hardworking," "demonstrating the work ethic," "eager," "successful," "happy," or even "just
wonderful." Many respondents expressed pride that their students
were from "diverse backgrounds," which leads one to believe that
they regard diversity as an important value in American education.
Indeed, very few mentioned student homogeneity as a plus, although
some cited having common values, such as "families are devoted to
education," as an important characterisitic.

Most schools in our sample served diverse student populations,
and the staff's expressions of pride focused more on what they felt
they had given their students than on what the students brought into
the school.

> The typical students at the RCA/YDC School have failed in
> the public school system. Many have been expelled from pub-
> lic schools. Most arrive here with reading levels below their
> grade levels. The students are all male, inner-city youths; many
> come from broken families. For the most part, they have been
> through the juvenile justice system and are incarcerated here.
> Some have been kicked out of other institutions. The students
> generally come socially maladjusted with little self-respect or
> respect for authority and with low self-esteem, but they are di-
> ametrically different when they leave.
> — GE-RCA Development School, Bensalem, Pennsylvania

*2. Schools with high public confidence were characterized by a
lively yet orderly environment and a caring and cooperative climate.*
It is difficult to attribute these general characteristics to specific persons or features in the schools; but to an outside observer, they are
what give the schools their unique "personality."

41

An atmosphere of controlled freedom provides an opportunity in this planned educational environment for students' social, physical, intellectual and aesthetic development.
— Brookland Junior High School, Washington, D.C.

The school is small enough to operate with an atmosphere of "family," yet large enough to offer the vast majority of students a well-rounded, comprehensive education. The school's ethos, while difficult to describe, is nonetheless the most unique aspect of the institution. Repeatedly, visitors have commented that they can really "feel" that Clayton High School is a fun place, yet at the same time they "feel" students are all business in the classrooms.
— Clayton High School, Raleigh, North Carolina

3. Teachers in these schools were described as well-prepared, competent, and caring about their students. These teachers are concerned about both cognitive and affective outcomes. They eschew narrow definitions of the teaching role and willingly accept the responsibility to reach their students through many avenues.

Our faculty is very close. Many of them live in this attendance area and display almost a family-type relationship.
— Root Elementary School, Fayetteville, Arkansas

The staff is a caring group of people who frequently go "above and beyond" for the benefit of students — often without informing administrators. Teachers are "child centered," yet they hold high academic expectations that have been reinforced by present and former administrative expectations.
— Albion Junior High School, Strongsville, Ohio

The staff has been described as unique. They care; they are concerned professionals and take their responsibility seriously.
— Kearney Junior High School, Kearney, Nebraska

4. School personnel in these schools saw their communities as supportive and deserving of high levels of service. Schools in our sample were in all types of communities — cities, suburbs, small towns, and rural areas — and served rich, poor, and mixed student populations; but the respondents saw their own community in a positive light.

Despite the limited economic circumstances of most families, the community overtaxes itself to provide its children with quality education. East Cleveland is one of the few communities in Ohio that has never rejected a school bond issue or operating levy.
— Chambers Elementary School, East Cleveland, Ohio

42

Ours is a community where nurturing education is important. High expectations are the rule in this community. Our staff's rising to these expectations is a credit to their education, experience, dedication, and effectiveness.

— Ames Senior High School, Ames, Iowa

Our affiliation with Queens College lends an air of legitimacy to the programs and provides us with additional personnel (student teachers, teacher-interns, professors) with which to innovate, remediate, enrich, and augment the program.

— Louis Armstrong Middle School
Elmhurst, Queens, New York

5. These schools reported that their curriculum is diverse and their instruction is varied in order to meet many different interests and abilities. Curriculum and instruction in these schools reflect a concern for student learning and for the conditions necessary for helping more students to learn and to learn more.

We are proud of our college preparatory curriculum, which is traditional but flexible. We offer a basic curriculum (language arts, math, sciences, foreign languages, social studies) supplemented with art, music, journalism, etc. We are attuned to the demands of the 80's, and make every effort to respond to these demands. For instance, we have recently provided every Lower School classroom with its own computer.

— Charlotte Latin School, Charlotte, North Carolina

Every student at Worthington High School must carry at least five courses during our seven-period day each semester. In other words, no student may carry more than one study hall per day per semester with one period for lunch. This requirement sets a high standard for students and communicates to parents that Worthington High School students will have to work hard at their courses. This requirement has been met with support from students, parents, and staff alike.

— Worthington High School, Worthington, Ohio

Attitudes and Values that Characterize
Schools with High Public Confidence

School personnel responding to our questionnaire attributed the high confidence they enjoyed to certain attitudes and values that permeated their schools. Although some attitudes and values were cited as general attributes of school climate, they usually reflected actions

43

of key persons in the school. In categorizing questionnaire responses dealing with attitudes or values, we have tried, whenever possible, to attribute them to the person(s) who expressed the attitudes or values.

1. The school climate reflected positive attitudes toward students, other people, learning, and achievement.

> Oh, I like this school. The first day I brought my boy here from the other school you could feel the difference. You know, Welcome — it's an attitude that's all over the place.

2. Teachers in these schools exhibited commitment and caring attitudes; they had confidence in themselves and their students.

> We have an excellent, caring group of teachers and other staff members. They work well with children and parents.
> — Genoa Junior High School, Genoa, Ohio

> High expectations for the staff have created a sense of professional pride resulting in a devoted and stable faculty.
> — Albion Junior High School, Strongsville, Ohio

> The teachers won't allow anyone to teach here who doesn't believe these kids can learn.
> — Marsalis Elementary School, Dallas, Texas

3. Students in these schools were proud of their school, respectful to visitors, enthusiastic about learning, and willing to work. Although the school in our sample served students from all types of backgrounds, school personnel reported that the students valued learning, had good work habits, exhibited self-discipline, were courteous, and seemed to appreciate the school's efforts on their behalf.

> Vandalism is almost nonexistent. No cigarettes have been lit in the building in over five years. Students respect the building and in turn are given the respect due them.
> — Soldotna Junior High School, Soldotna, Arkansas

> Columbia's high school students traditionally score well on national tests and have received numerous special recognitions. While national SAT scores were on the decline in recent years, Columbia students have consistently improved their scores. Each year several students from Columbia's two high schools, Hickman and Rock Bridge, are recognized as National Merit finalists and National Council of Teachers of English Award winners. Hickman High School boasts the largest number of Presidential Scholars of any high school in Missouri.
> — Columbia Public Schools, Columbia, Missouri

As we visited schools in the course of our study, we had an opportunity to experience firsthand the positive student attitudes that were described in the questionnaires. Students greeted us with poise, welcoming us and directing us to our destination. What distinguished them from students in many other schools was their ability to talk eloquently with adults about their school as a whole; they were knowledgeable and informative — even effusive — as they talked about a school that they obviously considered theirs. In classes, they were eager participants rather than passive recipients as they engaged in the process of learning.

> A student who is happy with school, who is experiencing success and is gaining personal and public recognition, is the best advertisement the school system can have. Students' attitudes about themselves and their school are exhibited in their behavior. A positive self-image projected by students helps the public to form a similar image of the school they attend.
> — Princeton High School, Princeton City School District Cincinnati, Ohio

> The students on the playground chatted with us. They didn't grunt or hang their heads. Inside the school, they talked more articulately than most adults do, and they were proud of their school. I asked one little girl, "Who braided your hair?" She said, "I did. Who tied your tie?" Another student described the "Hall of Presidents" (a set of portraits displayed on the wall) in a way that made Disneyland's guides look like amateurs.
> — Visitor, Chambers Elementary School, East Cleveland, Ohio

4. These communities valued education, respected educators, and showed great loyalty to their schools. School personnel reported that their communities were supportive of education in general and of the school's efforts in particular. The responses convey a feeling of mutual respect between school personnel and community members.

> A community is known by the schools it keeps.
> — Shaker Heights School District, Shaker Heights, Ohio

> In a community opinion survey, 22% of the respondents graded our schools an "A" and 45% graded them a "B." In the same survey, 74% of the respondents believed good public schools were very important in attracting new residents to Virginia Beach.
> — Virginia Beach City Public Schools, Virginia Beach, Virginia

45

Our community has supported a low pupil-teacher ratio in spite of declining enrollment.
— Katahdin High School, Sherman Station, Maine

5. Parents were supportive partners in the school's educational endeavors. Respondents reported that parents valued education and supported the school's efforts. Parent-school relations were close and trusting with practically no hostility or wary caution.

Parent involvement has been, and is, an ongoing part of being a member of the Hughes family. Parents equipped the first lounge for teachers in Tucson in 1931 and paid for the first elementary school librarian before the district provided one. Currently, parents sponsor and serve as leaders of eight scout troops at the school. Virtually 100% of the children had one or more parents attend the parent-teacher conferences last year.
— Sam Hughes Elementary School, Tucson, Arizona

Taft was almost closed, but due to strong parental support the school remained open.
— Taft Middle School, Albuquerque, New Mexico

6. Principals in these schools were open, warm, competent, and supportive of students, parents, and staff. The principal's values and attitudes were reported as important factors in the life of the school. These principals exhibited attitudes similar to those reported in the effective schools (see Stedman 1985, 1987; Robinson 1983; Lightfoot 1981, 1983; Goodlad 1983; and Peters and Austin 1985).

The principal *cares* about people and learning. We cannot make a carer out of a non-carer, can we? That would seem to be the superintendent's job — to select carers.
— Meadowlane Elementary School, Phenix City, Alabama

The average wage is very low in this area. I just looked around when I came here as a teacher and I saw all these kids from welfare homes. And I looked at them and thought, "These kids deserve as good an education as those who go to Princeton." So, we try to give it to them.
— Principal, Higginsport Elementary School, Higginsport, Ohio

Effective Practices Reported for Winning Public Confidence

Respondents were asked to describe activities and practices in their schools that made them unique, that were designed to promote public confidence, or that might contribute to the reputation of the school.

46

These schools made extraordinary efforts to foster parental involvement. They communicated frequently with parents and the broader
community. They initiated numerous ways to help students who might
"fall between the cracks" in other schools, and they provided a spectrum of engaging curricular and instructional practices. Their management techniques were participatory and involving, including enlisting
many non-parents into their activities. They also reported a high
proportion of students engaged in a wide variety of extracurricular
activities. These activities and others reported by schools are discussed in greater detail in the next chapter.

Chapter Seven
The Educative School:
Activities Reported by Schools
with High Public Confidence

As we analyzed the practices reported by the schools in our sample, it became apparent that they were doing the same types of things that had characterized schools with good discipline (PDK Commission on Discipline 1982). What we have found is that good schools tend to exhibit common characteristics that relate to good discipline, high achievement, positive staff morale, and public confidence (compare Wayson et al. 1988; Stedman 1985, 1988; Corcoran and Wilson 1986; and Murphy 1985).

In this chapter we have organized the practices found in schools with high levels of public confidence under the same eight factors we found in schools with good discipline. Our various studies leave little doubt that what good schools do includes some combination of these eight factors; and no school can be good without attending to most of them. In discussing these eight factors in schools with high public confidence, we give illustrative verbatim quotations from the school people themselves. In combination, these eight factors can serve as starting points for other schools to consider when planning how to build public confidence.

1. Staff members in good schools work together to solve problems and to improve the learning environment and outcomes.

The school staff regularly meets in teams to develop a consistent approach to student behavior. Much emphasis is placed on careful planning for instruction and the delivery of lessons. Most meeting time is devoted to developing solutions. Little, if any, time is spent on pointless complaining.
— Stowe Middle School, St. Louis, Missouri

When anyone here speaks of staff, they mean secretaries, custodians, cooks, teachers, and administrators. Everyone has input and is involved in the decision-making process.
— Kearney Junior High School, Kearney, Nebraska

High-confidence schools recognize problems, address them openly, and work to find solutions. Staff members and administrators are not defensive; instead, they admit mistakes, celebrate success, and constantly try to make things better.

The administration of Clayton High School identified key problems, which served as a rallying point for members of the community to become involved in solving. Dropout prevention and library facilities were the two problems. By openly sharing our concerns, it helped parents, business leaders, and other community members to develop a better understanding of the school and a sense of ownership.
— Clayton High School, Raleigh, North Carolina

The willingness of the school to provide parents and the community with information, to make changes where they were indicated, and to deal honestly with all the issues. This has gone a long way toward establishing a bond of trust between community and school, which is necessary to garner public support for education.
— Ellington High School, Ellington, Connecticut

High-confidence schools involve people who share a sense of purpose and mission and are eager to help each other accomplish that mission.

The public feels confident in what we are about because we also feel confident. Our school has a strong sense of mission guided by capable people in key leadership positions, from the central office to the classroom.
— Booker T. Washington High School, Tulsa, Oklahoma

We feel that goal setting, good instruction, and communication are the three important ingredients for attaining a high lev-

el of public confidence in our school. These are tools that any school can employ, but it takes a lot of time and effort and especially cooperation to develop skills among the faculty and staff.
— Meadows Elementary School, Sugar Land, Texas

Schools with high levels of confidence pursue clear objectives worked out jointly with the community. The community knows what the school is doing and what to expect from the school. In like manner, school personnel know what is expected and strive to meet those expectations.

Annual district goals provide the framework with which we monitor the important components of the school program and establish future directions for the district. A comprehensive goal-setting process is used to insure that the goals represent important priorities for the school and its community. Potential goals are initially generated at a faculty meeting and shared with the community at large. At a specially designated board of education meeting, administrators and board members are paired to screen and prioritize goals through a weighting process. The resulting four or five goals developed each year receive broad support because of the involvement that links the community and school in partnership.
— Hanover High School, Hanover, New Hampshire

2. Staff members in good schools involve more people in making decisions that govern the school and the learning within it, and they eliminate the status barriers that inhibit communication between persons or groups. High-confidence schools practice shared governance and problem solving. Students, staff members, administrators, parents, and community members participate in making decisions, planning, implementation, and evaluation.

Sharing the governance of the school with the community is one of the most positive actions at South High School. A 15-member School-Community Council, which has direct access to the Board of Education, participates in decisions affecting such areas as new course offerings, reductions in staff, curriculum revision needs, instructional implications from test scores, establishment of accelerated classes and remedial classes, and development of discipline procedures and policies. It also acts as liaison to community agencies and serves as a sounding board for the community.
— South High School, Salt Lake City, Utah

50

> We use consensus decision-making so that the winner-loser syndrome is avoided. Everyone's opinions are valued — students, parents, and staff.
>
> — Venado Middle School, Irvine, California

High-confidence schools foster leadership qualities in everyone in the school. From superintendent to building administrators to staff and students, they all step forward to provide leadership in accomplishing the school's goals.

> The single critical factor for generating confidence in the public schools of this district is the leadership ability of the superintendent. His high standards and equally high expectations have been communicated to all personnel. As a result of his intense leadership style and continued prodding and reinforcement, the expectation and desire for excellence has become almost self-generating. Students, teachers, parents and retirees — the entire educational community — know that the schools are great and expect them to continue in this tradition of excellence.
>
> — Roscommon High School, Roscommon, Michigan

> Administrators have to foster a healthy respect for teachers as capable professionals and have to turn over a good bit of decision making to them. You do not have to change the whole governance structure, but the superintendent does need to put the life of the school district into the hands of the principals and the teachers and then must rely on the recommendations that come out of that relationship.
>
> — Winnetka Public Schools, Winnetka, Illinois

> Students vote for the Outstanding Teacher Awards and for the school newspaper's Student-of-the-Month Awards. Students have been instrumental in deciding cafeteria menus and in conducting activities that provide positive reinforcement for student achievements.
>
> — Hoover Middle School, Albuquerque, New Mexico

Principals are key figures in these schools. They devote much time and effort to clarifying purposes, modeling norms, reinforcing best practices, and enlisting others to contribute to the school's success. These administrators are strong leaders, but they are not autocrats. They know that leadership depends on their ability to mobilize others. They do this through the strength of their personality, their demonstrated competence, and the example they set.

The principal works at keeping informed and he shares his information. He sets an example by fulfilling his responsibilities to his community and school and expects parents, teachers, and students to fulfill their responsibilities.

> — Meadowlane Elementary School, Phenix City, Alabama

The principal and assistant principal are actively and meaningfully engaged in the daily running of the school. They are highly visible, know all the students by name, and constantly visit the classrooms.

> — Wooster Intermediate School, Stratford, Connecticut

The principal and the other administrators work! I've never seen administrators who work so hard. When they work so hard, we just naturally want to keep up the pace.

> — Eastmoor High School, Columbus, Ohio

Schools that earn high levels of public confidence recognize and reward all who are putting forth extra effort and doing a good job. These schools do not reserve recognition for only a few "stars"; every child and every staff member who fulfills any responsibility, no matter how insignificant, is recognized.

> Sincere praise should be given whenever possible to the staff for the job they are doing. There should be time to laugh and time to listen to the staff's personal and professional concerns, and then act on those concerns.

> — Boones Creek Elementary School, Gray, Tennessee

Staff give a "ROEHMGRAM" to students who have done an above-average job in some school activity, such as improving one's grade or helping a teacher to organize an activity.

> — Roehm Junior High School, Berea, Ohio

Schools that earn high public confidence celebrate diversity among their students and in their communities. Most of these schools and districts served populations of mixed socioeconomic and ethnic backgrounds. These schools saw the mixture as an educational asset. Pride in these differences was evident in hallway decorations, classroom discussions, and school communications.

> We are a court-ordered, desegregated school with about 40% of our students bussed in from Guadalupe. Our students are from two distinct communities: Tempe and Guadalupe. About 80% of our students come from families where both parents work or from one-parent families with that parent working. A num-

ber of our students who come from Guadalupe do not read or speak English.
— Aguilar Elementary School, Tempe, Arizona

Although we qualify as a Chapter I school because of a high percentage of low-income families, we have as many students in our gifted program as our Chapter I Reading and Math programs.
— Doctors Inlet Elementary School, Doctors Inlet, Florida

3. Staff in good schools make every student feel that he or she belongs in the school and is served well by it.

The school is run with the idea that school is for the students. Student problems are not ignored whether it is a broken locker, a locker combination change, or class schedule changes.
— Mobridge Junior High School, Mobridge, South Dakota

Students in schools with high levels of confidence exhibit pride and a sense of ownership in their school. They are poised and confident in their interaction with both staff and visitors to the school. Their responses to visitors' questions indicate that they are knowledgeable about the school's goals. One sees little hostility, subservience, or apathy. Traffic in hallways is orderly but not regimented. Participation in classroom activities and discussions is enthusiastic, even passionate at times. Students seem to be alert and interested.

When walking the halls, you can feel the enthusiasm of the students.
— Kearney Junior High School, Kearney, Nebraska

As students leave school each day, they take their feelings with them, which they express directly and indirectly to parents, neighbors, and the community. As a result of the positive behaviors demonstrated by the students, this community is seeing a change in the school.
— Jefferson Davis Junior High School, Jacksonville, Florida

It would be a mistake to attribute the positive behaviors exhibited by students in these schools only to home influences. We observed these behaviors in schools in all types of communities, ranging from remote rural areas to the inner city. We firmly believe that such behaviors are *one of the schools' products*, which are both a symbol and an instrument of these schools' success. Clearly, the schools help them become that way. One might say that the school climate brings out the best in students, or perhaps it permits students to be what

53

they are capable of being. From our observations, we can only conclude that success in these schools stems largely from the quality of interpersonal relationships fostered within them.

Schools that enjoy high levels of community confidence feature students' accomplishments. These schools use tangible ways of letting students know they are important and have done a good job. Student products are displayed around the school and in the community; students and staff can look around and see that they count. Students are frequently "on stage" at all kinds of events that bring classmates, parents, and others together in the building.

> Children's academic and artistic work is professionally displayed in halls and classrooms and in school-produced literary publications. The children and parents take great pride in seeing their poetry, prose, and artwork exhibited next to the works of local professional and amateur artists.
> — Montezuma Creek Elementary School
> Montezuma Creek, Utah

> Nothing helps "sell" a school more than a strong tangible product which shows off student efforts. Student publications do just that.
> — Camden High School, Camden, South Carolina

> An Awards Assembly is held each nine weeks to honor students for high achievement and/or outstanding effort. When parents see those achievement and effort ribbons coming home, they know something is happening at school.
> — Oak Park Elementary School, Tampa, Florida

High-confidence schools provide opportunities for students to have real responsibilities and to make real contributions to their school and the community. They recognize the importance of developing student responsibility and use it to the school's advantage.

> The student government is totally responsible for the development of an annual $40,000 budget and negotiates with the coaches on how this budget is to be spent.
> — Olympia High School, Olympia, Washington

> The Hawthorne Publishing Company is a writing center operated by a teacher and librarian, where children are encouraged to write and publish their books. Parent volunteers help type the books, sew the pages together, and make bindings for the books.
> — Nathaniel Hawthorne Elementary School
> University City, Missouri

Schools with high public confidence demonstrate that they care about students. "Caring" was the word used most frequently in the program descriptions given to us for both elementary and secondary schools. School personnel exhibited caring in their interactions with both students and parents.

> The opinion in our community is that Wheeling Junior High is not a school that intimidates people but a place that cares about its students and parents. People are helped here, and our community knows that we are available at all times to lend assistance.
> — Wheeling Junior High School, Wheeling, West Virginia

> The caring attitude of our teachers contributes to the success of their students and is the most important thing we have going for gaining public confidence.
> — Clear Creek Secondary School, Idaho Springs, Colorado

High-confidence schools monitor each student's progress and provide for special needs whenever necessary. They communicate clear and accurate information to parents and involve them in the decisions made about their children, but they do not expect parents to do the school's work. Parents feel that the school knows and cares about their children and is taking care of their instructional needs.

> Our philosophy is based on the idea that a school should offer a program that meets the individual needs of students academically, socially, emotionally, and physically. In addition, we realize that children learn at different rates; and these differences should be viewed as assets and not liabilities. Our curriculum allows children to work in multi-age groups at their own pace.
> — Memphis State University Campus School
> Memphis, Tennessee

> Our bi-weekly student monitoring system is implemented using a computer or detailed tallying of teacher reports on students needing academic assistance. Vital to the system's success is the teachers' willingness to prepare the needed paperwork and the commitment of staff to work with and to encourage the students. Explaining the purpose of the monitoring system to students and their parents communicates the message that the school is concerned with academic success. And academic success improves public confidence in the schools; the public gets the message that we really do care about the students!
> — Princeton High School, Cincinnati, Ohio

High-confidence schools express their pride in a visible way through symbols, slogans, mottoes, and special programs.

> Develop a positive slogan and use it, mean it, and become it.
> — Soldotna Junior High School, Soldotna, Arkansas

> We give 110 percent effort each day to live up to our school mottoes, "Striving for Excellence" and "Best in the West."
> — Aguilar Elementary School, Tempe, Arizona

> The slogan "West is Best" is not only a chant at athletic contests but an attitude held by the entire school community.
> — Parkway West High School, Ballwin, Missouri

4. Staff members in good schools consider discipline to be a set of precepts or behaviors to be learned; and if they have not been learned, staff members teach them primarily by engaging students in the norms governing school life. Schools that earn high public confidence create a stable, predictable, and welcoming atmosphere that frees people to do their best creative work.

> It is this blend of business and pleasure that makes students feel welcome and at home and eager to be part of the organization.
> — Bishop Hendricken High School, Warwick, Rhode Island

> The students are involved in a warm, friendly, gentle place where it is safe to question, probe, and, at times, fail.
> — Kadimah School, Buffalo, New York

> The general positive climate of the school is the product of mutual trust and respect among adults and students.
> — Terrace Hills Junior High School, Grand Terrace, California

> People tell us that they know Root is a quality school the minute they step into the building. They say there is a special feeling about this school — a feeling of both relaxed friendliness and of educational effectiveness.
> — Root Elementary School, Fayetteville, Arkansas

5. Staff members in good schools seek out and use curricula and instructional methods designed to reach all their students.

> Our school uses a variety of teaching styles to meet the needs of our students. We have team-teaching in Grades 1, 3, and 6 in semi-open classrooms. We have self-contained classes in Grades K, 2, 4, 5, with teachers re-grouping students in the same grade level.
> — Aguilar Elementary School, Tempe, Arizona

High-confidence schools report a wide variety of extracurricular offerings in which large numbers of students participate. Although their basic academic programs are good and are expected to be good, these schools offer a wide range of extracurricular activities in response to student needs and interests. The schools and districts in our study reported from 70% to 90% of students engaged in extracurricular programs.

Although they need not be, extracurricular activities often are more engaging than the formal curriculum. In such activities students learn useful information, practice what they have learned, and receive immediate feedback from peers or coaches. The activities develop group cohesiveness and school spirit; they also help to establish closer relationships and more open communications among adults and students — all of which carry over into the classroom and have a positive affect on learning.

> We try to take advantage of any situation that will provide an outside experience for our students. For example, over the past year our students have received more than 20 full scholarships to Outward Bound programs. These have taken them from the Florida Keys to the mountains of western Maine.
> — Katahdin High School, Sherman Station, Maine

> Currently the school offers an alternative educational program. It also offers after-school programs in art, Spanish, calligraphy, recreation, chess, and tennis. All these activities are sponsored by the PTA and require parents to pay a fee, but scholarships are offered to those needing them.
> — Sam Hughes Elementary School, Tucson, Arizona

Schools with high levels of public confidence meet or exceed the community's expectations for academic achievement and other areas of performance. Of course, community expectations vary. A low socioeconomic community might not expect to send a high proportion of its graduates to college but does expect its schools to uphold a long tradition of preparing well-qualified graduates for local industries. As long as the school meets these expectations, it will enjoy public confidence among its constituents. If the school exceeds those expectations, as some have done in both rural and inner-city areas, the community holds the school in high regard and looks to educators as a major force for community development.

> What we do to build confidence in our school can work for anyone. Run a school where student achievement has a high

57

priority and let people know about it. Then take every opportunity to bring the adult community into your school to see for
themselves. Parent or not, they can and will be your best am-
bassadors of good will.

— Lincoln High School, Portland, Oregon

Schools with high levels of public confidence promote active inquiry rather than dull memorization of disconnected facts. Students
do learn facts; but they learn them in meaningful contexts, and they
practice applying them in new ways.

> Clovis took 40 out of 80 awards at the 1986 Science and En-
> gineering Fair. One of our students, Voon Wong, designed a
> system for recovering enzymes from soft drink sweeteners that
> would save $250 million a year if put into practice around the
> world. Another, Nancy Vu, designed a rabies test that can be
> returned within 48 hours rather than the normal two weeks we
> have to wait now.
>
> — Clovis West High School, Clovis, California

> We wanted to help children learn to express themselves in
> writing. We became concerned that putting so much emphasis
> on teaching cursive handwriting was detracting from real writing
> instruction. So we decided to delay cursive writing instruction
> until the fifth grade. To justify our decision, we subsequently
> conducted a study comparing the handwriting of all sixth-graders
> in our district with sixth-graders in another district. Neutral
> judges evaluated handwriting samples, and the results indicated
> that the cursive writing of our sixth-graders was significantly
> better than sixth-graders from the other district, even though
> ours had had only one year of instruction. At the same time,
> we compared teachers' attitudes toward teaching cursive writ-
> ing and found that our teachers had better attitudes than the other
> district's teachers. We concluded that we could teach cursive
> writing in a fraction of the time and with better teacher atti-
> tudes by waiting until the fifth grade.
>
> — Winnetka Public Schools, Winnetka, Illinois

High-confidence schools have well-developed goals and objectives
and monitor them to see that they are achieved. The school district
may have originally proposed these goals, but each school has lati-
tude for determining the means for achieving them and for sup-
plementing them with its own particular goals. The monitoring that
goes on seems more to assess how well the school as a whole is doing rather than to evaluate students.

The school district felt a need about five years ago to establish common district goals. This had a carry-over in our individual school. We develop general goals and also specific, measurable departmental goals at the beginning of each school year. Teachers develop and administer a pre- and post-test to determine whether the goals have been achieved in each subject area.

 — Annie Camp Middle School, Jonesboro, Arkansas

Our School Improvement Team, comprised of volunteer teachers, presents periodic workshops in areas where teachers say they need help, such as reading, counseling, discipline, etc. The School Improvement Team discusses our curriculum's strengths and designs strategies for working on areas needing improvement.

 — Hoover Middle School, Albuquerque, New Mexico

6. Staff members in good schools deal directly with students' personal problems before they manifest themselves in antisocial or delinquent behaviors. Schools with high public confidence take the time to orient new students and new parents to the school. Some publish a handbook for parents as well as for students and present it at the time of enrollment or at a home visit. These schools' handbooks go beyond the general information commonly found in handbooks. Some of them discuss the importance of quiet time and a place for students to study at home. Some contain information on job opportunities, selecting a college, and financing a college education.

Hoover conducts a "Little Brother/Sister" program. The incoming fifth-graders of our feeder elementary schools visit for a full school day with a Hoover student "pal." Hoover also has an orientation assembly for new students at the start of the school year, provides student handbooks, and uses parent aides as information assistants for new students.

 — Hoover Middle School, Albuquerque, New Mexico

These schools reported extensive orientation programs for introducing new parents to the school staff and provided time for informal discussions for parents to get to know the staff and to become informed about what the school is trying to achieve.

The school staff and the PTA provide an orientation session for parents new to the school. They are sent personal invitations to have lunch at school with the principal, vice principal, counselor, PTA representative, and Board of Education members. New parents can ask questions and voice their concerns.

 — Linden Elementary School, Oak Ridge, Tennessee

Children new to school spend two weeks prior to school opening in a "camp," with teachers from the school serving as "camp counselors." This helps to ease the transition into a new school situation.

— Louis Armstrong Middle School, Queens, New York

The principal makes personal calls in the evening to the homes of all new students after they have been enrolled a week or two to inquire about their adjustment to school.

— Hanford Secondary School, Richland, Washington

Many of these schools report special efforts to support students who might be facing severe personal problems that affect their school performance. Such efforts reflect these schools' acceptance of the professional responsibility of serving all students.

A high percent of our students come from divorced families. We have had special sessions for students from homes where a divorce has recently occurred.

— Aguilar Elementary School, Tempe, Arizona

Our district employs a full-time Drug and Alcohol Education Services Coordinator, who spends about 60% of his time in the high school. The coordinator conducts interventions, assists in arranging residential treatment placements, and leads inservice sessions for the district's staff. Our staff now feels confident in confronting students they suspect of having a drug or alcohol problem. Our students know they have someone who can really help them or someone they care about. And our parents know that the schools are willing to say that our community has a problem in this area, and that we are willing to provide resources to help.

— Worthington High School, Worthington, Ohio

High-confidence schools require and help staff members to develop as professionals and as people. These schools have extensive staff development opportunities to help staff become competent professionals.

We have set high standards for our staff as well as for our students, and we continually monitor our progress toward reaching the goals we have established. Our strong staff development program enables us to have high quality academic instruction.

— Cash Elementary School, Kernersville, North Carolina

A high level of professionalism is reflected by low staff absenteeism, continuous inservice training for upgrading skills, staff loyalty and dedication, and open communication.
— GE-RCA Development School, Bensalem, Pennsylvania

High-confidence schools counteract the impersonal character of institutional life by providing students with meaningful contacts with significant adults. Many adolescents in American high schools have little close personal contact with anyone other than peers. These schools recognize the isolation felt by many students and devise means to provide them with close contact with adults.

The U-32 High School assigns 12 student advisees to every adult in the school. These adults serve as parent surrogates, pressing students to do better work if pressure is needed and protecting them from any unfair treatment when they need an advocate. The students stay with the advisor all six years they are in school unless there is some personality conflict.
— U-32 High School, Montpelier, Vermont

7. *Staff members in high-confidence schools use the physical facilities in ways that enhance the learning environment and reinforce relationships.* These schools are attractive, clean, and welcoming. Both students and staff accept responsibility for keeping them that way.

Illing itself is a beautiful school. It provides a safe and aesthetically pleasing environment in which students and faculty can work. Visitors comment on how well it is kept, on the lack of vandalism, and on the beautiful display cases and bulletin boards throughout the building showing the activities going on within the brick walls.
— Illing Junior High School, Manchester, Connecticut

Students and parents are always greeted by clean, attractive surroundings. This does a great deal to set a positive tone for building constructive working relationships. Pride in our school and its appearance is encouraged from the first day of enrollment.
— Toussaint L'Ouverture Middle School, St. Louis, Missouri

High-confidence schools frequently use the school as a center for all types of community groups and activities.

West Junior High has become the community center of the area. It provides educational and recreational services for the entire community.
— West Junior High School, Colorado Springs, Colorado

Our building is used seven days a week for community education. Because of the way our custodial staff and our students take care of our building, many people are impressed by it. We are trying to get community education programs in our building while school is in operation. We want the non-parent taxpayer to see our school and meet our teachers and students. We also want the students to see that education is a lifelong process.
— Indian Hills Junior High School, Des Moines, Iowa

The school building is used six days a week with community education programs after school until 11:00 p.m. and on weekends.
— Soldotna Junior High School, Soldotna, Arkansas

8. Staff members in good schools relate well with parents and other community members, welcoming them into the school and into their classrooms and meeting them comfortably in their homes and their neighborhoods. They accent the positive but do not try to hide their problems when they exist. Principals may send "Happygrams" to students who have done something good for the school or brought the school recognition. Teachers may call a least one parent every day just to make some positive comment about a student and to answer any questions the parent may have.

There is a need for complete honesty with constituents in a school district. Identify your achievements and successes, but be sure that your problems are also pinpointed. When identifying problems, offer some possible solutions for eliminating the problem.
— Greenhills-Forest Park School District, Cincinnati, Ohio

An atmosphere of open dialogue and meaningful communication exists among students, parents, staff, and the Comsewogue community.
— Comsewogue Senior High School
Port Jefferson Station, New York

We write literally thousands of letters and cards to thank parents and visitors for anything they do that helps our school. We want people to know that we appreciate their help and effort.
— Aguilar Elementary School, Tempe, Arizona

Schools that earn public confidence almost invariably have a "cheerleader" on the staff. Many of the individuals who returned our questionnaires were cheerleaders; they were committed to the school, enthusiastic about its accomplishments, and undaunted by what had to be improved. Cheerleaders communicated the school's goals and purposes, modeled desired behaviors, stimulated others to contribute, complimented good performance, and lifted spirits when the going was tough. Many times they were administrators, but more often they were a "lieutenant" — a staff member who was loyal to the administrator and complemented the administrator's style.

The cheerleader frequently interacted informally inside the school and let the administrator maintain contacts outside the school. Cheerleaders spent much time on the phone to enlist contributions from staff or community members. They dropped encouraging notes in mailboxes and organized staff parties to bolster morale. Often working behind the scenes, they exhibited the "We can do it!" spirit that characterized so many of these schools and districts.

> Most of us are cheerleaders for the program, but I'd hate to think where we would be without Sarah. She never gives up. She lifts us up with a call, an idea, or a party — just when we need it most.
> — Kishwaukee Elementary School, Rockford, Illinois

Staff members in schools with high public confidence are sensitive to the needs of parents and the community. They are responsive to parents and provide them with a variety of information.

> The staff is readily available to discuss student progress and behavior concerns with parents. Our teachers make frequent phone contacts and home visits.
> — Coronado Hills Elementary School, Denver, Colorado

> Getting out and communicating with the community is critical. Tell them what's going on, be very open. If you've got something really messed up, admit it. Have the courage to be imperfect.
> — Pasco Senior High School, Pasco, Washington

> The communication between the teachers and parents has increased and improved. Phone calls to parents to report a child's progress, our open house, and our parents' night have given parents the feeling that they belong and that they can come to the school to get the help that they want.
> — Wooster Intermediate School, Stratford, Connecticut

> We are appalled that teachers in some places won't schedule a late conference with parents who really cannot come at any other time. Teachers and administrators should be available to parents.
> — Woodland Hall Academy, Tallahassee, Florida

63

Schools with high confidence emphasize a strong role for parents in educating their own children. School personnel want parents to know how they can help their youngsters get the most out of school. One school makes videocassette lessons for students to take home and do with their parents. This gives parents a better understanding of the instructional program and guides them in helping their children with homework.

> On a regularly scheduled basis, we write individual letters to some 25 parents (selected randomly) inviting them to come to the school on a scheduled day and spend a full (or part of a) day visiting classes and conferring with counselors, teachers, and administrators. This program has enabled us to win many friends and supporters for the school.
> — Brandywine High School, Wilmington, Delaware

Schools that enjoy high public confidence employ some form of monitoring public opinion. Many of the districts conduct periodic surveys to assess community concerns and attitudes. They sometimes poll different groups in the community. Some schools use more informal procedures in open meetings or in discussion sessions. Others may use a mail survey or send surveys home with students. However it is done, schools with confidence listen to, and seek to respond to, their publics.

> Our telephone survey to a scientific sample of more than 500 citizens showed that the people think we offer a quality program, emphasize the basics enough, assign enough homework, encourage students to do well, graduate students with enough skills, and have adequate discipline. Overcrowding was identified as our worst problem this year. We are concerned about the 12% who felt that students could not get extra help.
> — Fairbanks North Star Borough School District, Alaska

> The principal has made a point of becoming very active in community activities and programs. This visibility gives him the opportunity to deal with perceptions the public may have and to speak of the school's accomplishments.
> — Port Chester High School, Port Chester, New York

These schools report frequently to their publics in a variety of formal and informal ways to let them know what the schools are doing and how they are responding to community concerns. Many of these schools have a newsletter, which is disseminated in a variety of ways. Some are mailed home; some are sent home with students. Some schools use hi_hly creative ways of getting information about the schools to the total community, not just parents of school-age children. One principal gave each child four magnets with instructions for using them to display their schoolwork on the refrigerator door. Students with newspaper routes leave a copy of the school newsletter when they deliver their papers. Copies are left at banks, beauty parlors, and barber shops — anywhere that people are likely to gather. One school reported printing the school news on placemats, which then were placed in the local restaurants.

> Communication is maximized by newsletters, frequent meetings, newspaper articles, etc. Administrators and teachers call parents frequently to report positive information as well as concerns.
> — Bayport-Blue Point District #5, Bayport, New York

> A booth at the shopping center staffed by school personnel provides the public with information about the schools without the public having to come to the school. The booth is open on Saturdays and features a different topic each week, such as reading, vocational education, special education, or the school lunch program. A sign on the booth says, "Columbia Public Schools Meet the Public — Today's Topic of Emphasis is Reading."
> — Columbia Public School District, Columbia, Missouri

> We have a media program that makes extensive use of the cable television network throughout the city. We originate the television programs, which feature live music, sporting events, fine arts performances, and talent shows. We have a large percentage of our student body involved in various activities.
> — Kickapoo High School, Springfield, Missouri

Schools with public confidence involve parents and community members in a variety of ways. They do not just encourage it; they plan for it by actively seeking ways to get people into the school for many purposes. Community members use their skills to teach mini-courses or conduct craft fairs. Volunteers help with clubs devoted to both academic interests and hobbies. Some serve as officials at tournaments. Some community members serve only as a supportive audience at curricular and extracurricular events, but their presence is always welcomed.

> The public's perception of the schools is positively influenced by aggressively involving the community in the school and by

giving high visibility to the accomplishments of the staff and the students.

— George Mason Junior-Senior High School
Falls Church, Virginia

We have nearly 200 adult community members involved in a direct relationship with the school on a regular basis.

— Brandywine High School, Wilmington, Delaware

Once it became evident to teachers that involving parents provided them with new skills and resources, a parent-liaison system was organized to handle the growing number of requests for parent aides. The teachers realized that the parents' presence provided the home-school partnership that schools with high public confidence must have.

— Hoover Middle School, Albuquerque, New Mexico

High-confidence schools make use of many advisory committees and task forces drawn from various sectors of the community.

The Citizens' Advisory Committee meets once each month. Forty or more parents meet with the administrative team to discuss school problems and to seek solutions to these problems and lend parental support.

— Brandywine High School, Wilmington, Delaware

The school discipline procedure was developed with the consensus of the school's community, staff, students, and administrators.

— Terrace Hills Junior High School, Grand Terrace, California

High-confidence schools encourage older citizens to visit often. Some schools give free passes for student performances of plays, musicals, and concerts; also debates, art shows, spelling bees, and other student programs. This simple effort ensures the school of an appreciative audience while at the same time providing entertainment and companionship for retired citizens. The free passes say to older people, "We want you to come to our school and see what we are doing."

Our community is getting older. Fewer adults have children in our school; yet, we rely on the entire community for the tax money to support our school. We have instituted special programs to attract older members of the community and to keep them involved with programs. We have a Grandparents Day where each student invites a grandparent to school; or if the student doesn't have a grandparent nearby, then some older person in the community that the young person knows well and likes is invited. We show them around the school and have lunch together. At the conclusion of the activity, we present a photo of the students with their grandparents. We also provide passes to retired and older people in the community to attend school functions. In this way, even though they do not have youngsters in school, we can show them what is going on in school and some of the benefits our school offers to the community. We have never had a budget rejected or a bond issue voted down.

— Linden School, Oak Ridge, Tennessee

Golden Opportunity Passes are issued to citizens over 62 years of age so that they may attend student events at no cost. The district personnel presented a musical version of "Scrooge" as a Christmas gift to the community.

— School District of Superior, Superior, Wisconsin

Parents are invited to eat lunch with their children during the year. Grandparents are invited for a "Special Day."

— Bayport-Blue Point District #5, Bayport, New York

High-confidence schools provide valuable services to the community in the form of entertainment, education, and volunteer work.

In Home Economics we have a co-op program for our catering class, which involves working with our school cafeteria. This program gives students job training in commercial food service. Eighteen students plan, prepare, and serve food for various school and community functions.

— South Plantation High School, Plantation, Florida

Our students provide a valuable community service, which entails life-threatening situations, when they serve on the Ellington Volunteer Ambulance team during school hours. They were featured for their work on the ABC Network program "That's Incredible." Our students present a very positive image to the community, not only for themselves but also for their school.

— Ellington High School, Ellington, Connecticut

Students often serve as volunteers for the Special Olympics meets. They assist at nursing homes and centers during the holidays and other times. Community service is a major function of our service clubs.

— Plantation High School, Plantation, Florida

Schools with high levels of public confidence have an open and cooperative relationship with the local media. They see the media as partners, and they cooperate by providing the media with access to needed information for stories and sometimes even prepare stories for the media.

> We cannot rely solely on the local press to write about our program. Our public relations program involves virtually the entire community. Local newspapers, the principal's newsletter, board programs, our special public relations presentations, our outside bulletin board, our special publications, and our recorded messages relate news about our school and bring the success of the students to the eyes of the public.
> — Northern Valley Regional High School
> Demarest, New Jersey

> The school is always willing to grant interviews and to provide information; we have found that our sincere comments on community educational matters have often led people to our school and others to react positively to our school. We believe our best publicity comes from pleased (not coddled) students and parents who have received more than what they anticipated when they selected our school.
> — Briarcrest Baptist High School, Memphis, Tennessee

Summary

After studying 500 schools with good discipline, more than 250 with reputations for excellence, and now more than 200 with high levels of public confidence, we feel confident in saying that the three areas are closely related. Even though we have conducted separate studies in these three areas, achievement, discipline, and public confidence cannot be separated when assessing schools as a whole. They should be viewed as reciprocals: good discipline contributes to high achievement and high achievement contributes to good discipline. Both, in turn, lay the groundwork for high public confidence.

Whatever schools do to earn the lable of "good" is manifested in four outcomes that educators have long sought: well-disciplined students and committed staffs, high achievement and other hallmarks of quality learning, high levels of staff morale, and public confidence. For too long educators have attempted to achieve these outcomes as individual efforts, when they can accomplish all four for the price of one.

Chapter Eight
What School Districts Do
to Gain Public Confidence

Individual schools with high public confidence can and do exist in mediocre or poor districts, but they are more likely to be found in school districts that have earned public confidence. The relationship is clear: these districts have created conditions and adopted policies that allow individual schools to do the kinds of things reported in the last chapter.

This chapter summarizes what 65 school districts told us about their efforts to win public confidence — sometimes in circumstances where confidence had reached an all-time low. These school districts include suburban, rural, and medium-size and large cities They serve students from all socioeconomic levels. The activities they reported seem independent of the wealth of the district. Generally, they reflect an educational philosophy characterized by: devotion to students, faith in the value of education, dedication to professional duty, commitment to civic responsibility, and resoluteness in improving education and the quality of community life.

School districts with high public confidence see their major role as one of developing and supporting schools that teach students and reach out to the community. They seem to know that public confidence depends primarily on the attitudes and actions of those who work most closely with students.

Our school program is a fortunate blend of a good curriculum, extracurricular activities, excellent teaching, and attention to individual differences. Many parents outside the district prefer to pay tuition to have their children attend the Clayton schools.
— Clayton Public Schools, Clayton, Missouri

Columbus Monthly ranked Worthington High School first among the suburban schools in overall quality. It concluded that for college-bound students there wasn't a stronger public secondary program in central Ohio. Perry Middle School was named one of the top schools in the nation in the federal recognition program. Worthington Hills Elementary was recommended by the state education department for similar recognition, and Colonial Hills Elementary was one of 100 "Good Schools" selected by Kappa Delta Pi in its study of exemplary schools.
— Worthington School District, Worthington, Ohio

Our teachers are also researchers, authors, editors, and staff developers. We look for intelligent, energetic people and then create a climate where they can add to our knowledge. We reward creative activity through increased opportunities for professional visibility and leadership. The climate and culture that exists in a school district ought to model the climate and culture that exists in a good classroom.
— Winnetka Public Schools, Winnetka, Illinois

Whatever we do is designed to give teachers every possible assistance in helping boys and girls get the maximum they can get from school. You have to model the behavior you want from your teachers: take criticism, attend inservice, work hard, celebrate successes, provide need-specific staff growth opportunities, focus on team effort with no individual grandstanding, and don't try to change any successful ways that are legal.
— SHAL Program, St. Louis Public Schools
St. Louis, Missouri

Districts with high public confidence win the confidence of their employees.

The rapport between administration and teaching staff is of fundamental importance to the school system. We shudder every time we see news reports of acrimony in other districts. What an experience for students, seeing their teachers and their school administrators at each other's throats! How lucky we are here where good intentions and common goals prevail. Everybody benefits. Families settle in this area largely because of the good school situation.

— Columbia School District, Columbia, Missouri

High-confidence districts communicate frequently with their publics and focus on what students are doing.

One form of communication is the Superintendent's Newsletter, which is sent to parents and key communicators in the community every 4½ weeks. The newsletter is sent along with progress reports and report cards, as is the Principal's Newsletter from the students' school. A special edition of the newsletter is included as an insert in the district's adult education brochure, which is mailed to all residents twice a year. An annual report highlighting the year's accomplishments and reviewing the district's financial status also is sent to parents, key communicators, and the media. A fact brochure, data sheet, and boundary maps are provided to area realtors and the Chamber of Commerce for distribution.

— Township High School District 211, Palatine, Illinois

Real estate agents must be kept current on the highlights of the school district. A school representative is available to speak to realtors at their sales meetings. These are usually held once per week. Allowing the realtors to ask questions about the schools often flushes out rumors and allows the school representative to clarify many issues. These people are often the ones who can give the greatest credibility to the schools as they talk with clients, neighbors, and friends. Distributing printed materials at these meetings has proven most successful.

— Princeton City School District, Cincinnati, Ohio

Districts with high public confidence have the confidence of the local media. The media are the only source of information about the schools for many in the community. Several districts in our study sent us copies of community surveys they had conducted, which consistently showed that about 25% of their constituents received most of their information about the schools from the media, particularly newspapers. A hostile media can create a mindset in the public that is difficult to overcome. High-confidence school districts maintain good relationships with media representatives, particularly print media, which carry more information about schools than the electronic media.

We believe the education reporter and editor of our local paper should not be considered as adversaries but rather as partners

in establishing an atmosphere of openness. Besides being invited to all school board meetings, our education reporter has been invited to many large and small group meetings where deliberations on future directions for our curriculum were discussed. This led, we believe, to a feeling of mutual trust and respect.
— Virginia Beach City Public Schools, Virgina Beach, Virginia

The local newspaper publishes a weekly "Teen Scene" page featuring student-written stories. The paper also publishes a "Creative Writing Corner" on a monthly basis. Informational packets are distributed to parents of all newborns in the local hospital; parents who enroll can receive follow-up packets on their children's birthdates through age four. Citizens whose efforts are recognized in the newspaper receive a congratulatory note from the school district. The school psychologists have written an information series in the local newspaper under the title, "Living with Children Is Easier When. . . ."
— School District of Superior, Superior, Wisconsin

Districts with high public confidence involve parents and other community members in planning, advising, and decision making that affects policy and practice.

After studying the programs in our schools, a 36-member task force worked for a year to develop a meaningful set of goals. They drew up a preliminary philosophy statement and a set of objectives, then presented them to a citizens' advisory group, a student advisory group, and groups of school personnel. After school board approval, the philosophy statement and set of goals became the guiding force for intensive curriculum changes.
— Virginia Beach Public Schools, Virginia Beach, Virginia

A wide range of committees at each school and districtwide offer residents the chance to become involved in school decisions. Committees include: Budget Committee, Building Construction Committee, Business Advisory, Career Education Advisory, Curriculum Advisory, Field Use Advisory, Special Education Advisory, and Student Rights and Responsibility Advisory.
— Tigard School District 23J, Tigard, Oregon

Districts with high public confidence use a large number of volunteers, usually to assist directly with instruction.

Every school in our district has a parent-teacher association. In addition we have a strong Volunteers-in-Education program in our school system. This year we have more than 4,300 volunteers helping in our 63 schools.
— Palatine Township High School District, Palatine, Illinois

We enjoy the talent of retired professionals with special expertise now living in the area. A retired IBM engineer and a retired aeronautical and mechanical engineer worked with high school students to construct a microcomputer and computer-controlled robot. A retired English professor works with a group of students to improve writing techniques. A local artist instructs upper elementary grades. Members of RSVP correspond regularly with first-, second-, and third-grade students; at the end of the year they meet with the children and share an afternoon. Other members of the community serve as high school tutors, and they come to be vocal supporters for those students and for the school. The local literacy council provides volunteer aides for new students for whom English is not their native language. The school district has a working relationship with the city school parks department, and all but the high school grounds and fields are open for public use under the supervision of park department employees.
— Bellingham School District, Bellingham, Washington

Districts with high public confidence have sound fiscal management and exhibit careful, but not miserly, stewardship over the community's money.

The Columbia School District has done it again. Faced with the tight budget conditions that are plaguing districts everywhere, school officials have come up with an average 9% teacher salary increase. It's not magic. The main ingredient in getting the raises for the teachers is strong budget management. Superintendent Thompson has scrounged for money. There's not the slightest doubt that our school officials sincerely want to pay teachers more and are held back only by financial restraints that the teachers can understand.
— Columbia School District, Columbia, Missouri

Districts with high confidence have intensive and purposeful staff development programs.

A staff development project, which will run over several years, was initiated last spring. A planning team of building administrators and Office of Instruction personnel developed

73

the staff development model known as the Instructional Skills Program. They worked with the teacher's advisory committee to polish the training sessions. The first to be trained were the building principals and the central office staff. Approximately 60 teachers will receive the same training a year later, with an additional 120 trained in each of the next two years, and so on until the entire instructional staff will be trained.

> — Williamsburg-James City County Public Schools
> Williamsburg, Virginia

Districts with high confidence give high priority to curriculum, instruction, and learning. Their students achieve well in academics and in other areas. In recent years they have responded to rising expectations for achievement in general and for improved outcomes for students who formerly were not expected to achieve. Many of these districts were ahead of national reform movements in developing and piloting models of instruction that other school systems have subsequently used.

> The district has made significant academic improvements, which, of course, have been reported to the public. These successes have raised confidence considerably. We know a PR program would do nothing for us if we had nothing to sell. Once our programs improved, we told the world just how good we are. Many good schools don't spread the word, and some less successful districts try to sell an "empty box." Credibility is important.
> — Galloway Township Public Schools, Smithville, New Jersey

> The instructional process in Duval County is based on a systematic approach to curriculum development, instructional materials adoption, classroom instruction, and evaluation. Curricula are developed by teachers during the summer session. Achievement in Duval County comes by design, not by chance. The results have brought recognition from all over the nation. For example, Englewood, Raines, and Ribault High Schools received Ford Foundation Awards for raising achievement, improving student life, increasing parent participation, improving discipline and attendance, and placing graduates in college. All of them have more than 30% minority enrollments. Those are only examples; the whole district has improved.
> — Duval County Public Schools, Jacksonville, Florida

> We meshed two philosophies to create a concept of the "Clovis Sparthenian," from the Spartans who valued physically sound

and disciplined bodies and the Athenians who valued artistic and intellectual pursuits. We developed a total curriculum dedicated to educating individuals who exemplify well-being in mind, body, and spirit. Lots of people say that, but we really mean it. For example, the "Sparthenian" curriculum in the cognitive areas focuses on understanding knowledge and using this knowledge in new situations. Remembering a fact is of little value unless you can use it to solve problems. Almost all of our Sparthenians consistently do better than average on achievement tests every year.

> — Clovis Unified School District, Clovis, California

Districts with high confidence establish programs that serve all of the students in the schools by meeting different needs and interests. Most of these districts in our study served communities with diverse populations. They stressed the positive values of having students from many cultural backgrounds; and they found success in bridging socioeconomic, ethnic, racial, or linguistic differences. Districts serving homogeneous, wealthy communities stressed academic achievement, college attendance, and successful competition with private schools; but they reported very diverse curricular and extracurricular offerings as well.

> Public confidence is found in school districts that have developed quality educational programs to meet the needs of diverse student populations. When the product of such school districts demonstrates competence in areas such as basic skills and college and vocational preparation, the public tends to view the schools favorably.
>
> — Columbia Public Schools, Columbia, Missouri

Districts with high confidence expect those who work directly with students to develop the means of achieving district goals and to overcome obstacles that inhibit achieving these goals.

> From the district level you focus on outcomes, not methods. Everything you want to accomplish must be done by those people in those schools.
>
> — SHAL Program, St. Louis Public Schools
> St. Louis, Missouri

> Administrators have to foster a healthy respect for teachers as capable professionals and have to turn over a good bit of decision making to them. You don't have to change the whole governance structure, but the superintendent does need to put

75

the life of the school district into the hands of the principals and the teachers.

— Winnetka Public Schools, Winnetka, Illinois

Districts with high confidence encourage leadership in schools and classrooms.

Every school employee shares the responsibility for improving public attitudes about our schools. Whatever position you hold, friends and relatives value your opinion and pay close attention to what you say. How visitors and callers to the school are received can set the tone for their feelings about our schools. A friendly voice on the telephone, a smile, and a willingness to listen can ease a potential confrontation into a productive discussion.

— from employees' handbook, *You Make the Difference* Pittsburgh Public Schools, Pittsburgh, Pennsylvania

Our superintendent, Jim Hyre, keeps beating us [the principals] over the head with the question, "Would you want your kid to be in this school?" Then he says, "If not, why not?" The "why" becomes my needs assessment. Now, I know that you must believe in the school. There are a whole lot of people who don't believe in you, in themselves, in the central office — they only believe that at the end of the month there will be a little something in the mailbox. The principal has to help them believe in themselves, that they are somebody and they are capable. I tell them: "If it is to be, it is up to me."

— Principal, Eastmoor High School, Columbus, Ohio

Districts with high confidence appoint competent, caring professionals throughout the school system.

Within the past five years, Austin teachers have been named the state's most outstanding in the areas of elementary science, high school science, foreign language, and physical education. Austin is the only school district in the state to have teachers named outstanding teacher in each of the four foreign languages we teach. We had high school teachers selected as "Distinguished Teacher" by the U.S. Department of Education, as a winner of the Presidential Award for Teaching Excellence in Mathematics and Science, as a winner of the State Bar Association's Award for Teaching Excellence, and as one of two finalists for the Teacher in Space program. Administrators were named most outstanding by eight different state and national groups.

— Austin Independent School District, Austin, Texas

The teachers in our district have far more training than the state or national average. They show a genuine interest in their students and have won many professional honors. They work after school hours to help students, serve on curriculum committees to improve the quality of education, and increase their teaching skills by enrolling in university courses.

— Emporia Unified Schools, Emporia, Kansas

Districts with high confidence select superintendents who are educational leaders who can gain community support.

In times of both declining student enrollment and serious financial constraints, this district has been able to achieve and maintain support from the community because of the strong leadership and management capabilities of the superintendent.

— Regional School District #13, Storrs, Connecticut

It would be impossible to estimate how valuable it has been for this district to have Jay Robinson as the superintendent. He brought the best educational leadership possible and was able to get the best from every person in the district. The district is immeasurably better in every conceivable way since he came here.

— Charlotte-Mecklenburg Public Schools
Charlotte, North Carolina

Districts with high confidence select outstanding principals and provide them with staff support.

You work with the principals, take them to see successful projects, and provide them with data about their schools. Then you provide the staff technical assistance that helps them design and plan instruction focused on individual student needs.

— SHAL Program, St. Louis Public Schools
St. Louis, Missouri

More than 200 administrators applied for the principalship at Malvern. Andreadis was our choice. At 30, he already had been headmaster, chief financial officer, and instructional leader at the Greek Cathedral School in New York. Before that, he was the assistant headmaster of the Dalton School — no slouchy place. He was completing a Ph.D. at Columbia; had taught science, math, and psychology; and had coached three sports. He looked like the kind of leader we want to have in our schools.

— Shaker Heights City School District, Shaker Heights, Ohio

Districts with high confidence conduct surveys or use other means to gauge community attitudes and concerns. And they use the results to develop policies and practices for resolving problems.

> We interviewed 350 parents and 150 non-parents and received a 60% return on questionnaires sent home with each child. Only one in 10 had negative feelings on how well we were doing. They agreed that teachers are the most important single element in the educational process, but thought they should be removed if they weren't really teaching. Two-thirds of the parents and just over half of the non-parents said they would support an increase in taxes. About four out of 10 thought we should improve discipline. We also learned that too few of them are aware of some important programs we have instituted.
> — Tucson Unified School District, Tuscon, Arizona

> For many years, a group of women called Key Communicators have conducted telephone surveys of residents on topics ranging from the district calendar to budget cuts to course offerings. The results from these surveys have helped the district to better understand community concerns.
> — Pattonville School District, St. Louis County, Missouri

High-confidence districts "sell" their schools, their programs, and their students.

> We want to create schools people want to do business with, schools that are sensitive to the marketplace. We want to improve the product from its initial conception through sale.
> — Macomb Intermediate School District, Macomb, Michigan

> The director, Richard Dodds, became concerned when he learned that 300 of our students had gone over to separate schools and the province was going to provide full funding for separate schools. He uses the slogan, "Our Schools Are Great Places To Be." Surveys showed that we had the oldest population and the biggest proportion of single-parent familes in the city; so, we increased continuing education courses and gave our spare space to day-care agencies. Since then, we have had a slight increase in enrollments for the first time in years.
> — East York Board of Education, Toronto, Ontario

Districts with high confidence have initiated partnerships with local businesses in recent years.

> A New Residents' Handbook was published in cooperation with the Board of Realtors. Anheuser-Busch, BASF, Colonial

Williamsburg Foundation, and Newport News Shipbuilding have assisted with staff development and management training. Fifteen area restaurants helped with a Tour of Excellent Restaurants, which raised more than $15,000 for scholarships.
> — Williamsburg-James City County Public Schools
> Williamsburg, Virginia

School-business partnerships are not all giving by the business partner. The district sends teachers to instruct employees who are working on their G.E.D. equivalency diplomas. Superintendent Geiger says, "We are looking for a long-term relationship — a marriage of business and schools." The idea has paid off. Smithville has contributed nearly $100,000. Caesars has provided free rooms for nearly two dozen educators conducting a four-day evaluation for the school system. Harrah's, Hanson's and Sons Construction Company, and MidLantic National Bank are some of the other sponsors.
> — Galloway Township Public Schools, Smithville, New Jersey

Many districts with high confidence have established foundations that provide funds for many activities not supported by taxes. The foundations foster public confidence by giving visibility to worthy programs needing extra funding. And those involved in the fund raising come to have a vested interest in these programs. Most of the funding for the school foundation comes from private subscription and donations, but some districts reported that their own employees make generous contributions as well.

> Lima City Schools Scholarship Fund provides about 50 small scholarships to graduates from the high school. The fund is financed by staff payroll deductions. Nearly one-fifth of the staff make regular monthly contributions. The whole operation is administered by an incorporated Scholarship Committee.
> — Lima City Schools, Lima, Ohio

Factors Eroding Public Confidence Reported by Schools and Districts

Even schools and districts that have earned public confidence can face circumstances that will erode that confidence. Following are some generalizations drawn from what representatives of these high-confidence districts said could cause a loss of confidence. Actions to lessen the impact of factors causing loss of confidence can be inferred from what these districts are doing.

Declining enrollment undermines confidence. With loss of enrollment comes building closures, teachers dismissals, and budget cutbacks, all of which cause uncertainty among staff members and in the community. Uncertainty undermines confidence.

> Several years ago, when an elementary school had to be closed because of structural deterioration, we did not have sufficient time to properly prepare parents for moving their children to a different school. The change was made in 24 hours and was disturbing to both students and parents.

> We lost the public's confidence a few years ago when program cuts were prompted by the recession and a cutback in state funds.

In high-confidence districts there was generally an effort to use staff and community involvement to get the "best" decision when faced with budget cuts or declining enrollments. Being able to make cuts without major community controversy was often cited as a sign that the public had confidence in the district.

Labor-management problems cause a loss of confidence. Respondents (mostly administrators) usually said that "unionism" caused communities to lose confidence, and that "strikes" always cause a loss of confidence. But their examples show that the real cause of loss of confidence is *conflict*.

> Public confidence takes a nosedive when unionization of teachers, administrators, and staff appears to be interfering with the delivery of solid, educational service to the students.

> There was a distinct loss of confidence in our district and other surrounding districts when teachers went out on strike about eight years ago. It took a span of two years to win back public confidence from parents and other community members. It was the one and only strike experienced in our district.

> Organizational conflicts with employee groups related to collective bargaining cause one side or the other to say things that are harmful to the district. Some districts lose confidence during negotiations because they seek confrontation rather than consensus.

These high-confidence districts avoided conflict through good personnel practices, involving staff members in problem solving and program development, and promoting higher professional status for teachers. Most respondents felt that negotiating contracts and handling labor problems without controversy enhanced public confidence.

Dissatisfied staff members' remarks to the community can undermine public confidence. Respondents reported that negative public comments from school personnel can sow seeds of concern in the community.

> Loss of confidence occurs most frequently when a member of the staff — from superintendent to custodian — speaks disparagingly about our school. Staff members who make public derogatory remarks about the school system and its programs are probably the greatest cause of loss of public confidence.

> Negative teacher comments made during negotiations cost us a loss of confidence when we were writing the last contract.

High-confidence school districts do not restrict the right of their personnel to speak publicly. Rather, they promote employee satisfaction and loyalty through fair treatment and involvement in setting district goals. Because they maintain an open, non-defensive stance when dealing with problems, the community knows that an occasional staff complaint will be dealt with in a fair and open manner.

Poor fiscal management reduces public confidence. Accusations or evidence of fiscal mismanagement, such as suspect expenditures, overspending, cutting expenditures for popular or basic programs, or cutting budgets as a political effort to show fiscal conservatism can stir a community to revolt.

> Confidence really dropped when we experienced financial problems and cutbacks in staff and programs and then found out the financial problems did not exist.

> Other districts (not ours) have lost public support by deficit spending.

High-confidence districts send frequent communications to the public about fiscal issues. Their use of sound business practices for accounting, auditing, awarding contracts, etc., tended to forestall any hint of fiscal mismanagement. Most also tried to hold costs or tax rates at less than the top for their region. In those districts that had the highest per-pupil expenditures and the highest teacher salaries, their communities had come to believe that they "get what they pay for." Because their schools could claim the best programs and student outcomes in the region, these communities clearly were getting what they paid for.

Conflict on the school board causes loss of confidence. Bickering, self-serving actions, special-interest pleading, and interpersonal conflicts in board meetings or in the public media reduces confidence in the schools.

> It is impossible to keep the public trust when the board of education or administration gets involved in politicking and not educating.

> Grandstanding by board members who have other political ambitions makes the public get itchy. They worry about their kids and about the public image of the city.

High-confidence districts try to avoid such problems by having sound procedures for developing school policy, by providing educational programs to serve all types of students, by involving broadly representative groups on advisory committees or task forces, by attracting educationally concerned candidates to the board, or by enlisting powerful economic and civic groups to take greater interest in school affairs. They provide inservice training for board members and keep them fully informed about school operations.

Conflict between the school board and the superintendent reduces public confidence. Conflict among decision makers at the top level ripples through the entire district, resulting in loss of confidence among school staff as well as in the community. Sometimes such conflict pits school personnel against the community; more often, it divides the community with different constituencies taking sides. School improvement efforts slow or even stop as school personnel wait to see who will "win," or which side is "safe" to support.

> School board and superintendent fights make the public think the left hand doesn't know what the right is doing. The whole district seems to stand still until it shakes out.

High-confidence districts seem to have less conflict at the top level, because an atmosphere of good will and trust has been built over time. When disagreements do arise, the parties involved consider the cost in public confidence and take steps to secure that confidence when the issue under contention is over.

Secretive or suspect decisions by school officials cause loss of confidence. Professionals can easily fall into a trap that has lead to the downfall of kings: the belief that they "know best" what their constituents need. Such arrogance can result in unanticipated community backlash.

> A credibility gap develops if a district promotes the success of its programs, but then people learn that there is no documen-

tation and the success was not real. This also applies to finances when the board of education says there is no money and then finds hundreds of thousands of dollars.

A failure to be honest with our public is the major failing of public schools. Support can evaporate completely if the public knows the schools are deliberately stretching or covering up information. When people do not know what is happening, they tend to believe those things which are negative and build on that.

Failure to follow policy can cause a whole lot of trouble, and saying one thing but doing another causes more.

High-confidence districts keep communication lines open to their constituents. When problems arise, they are communicated and steps are taken to resolve them. School officials know the sources and limitations of their power, but they maintain a sense of humility and cultivate the loyalty of community members through involvement and demonstrations of genuine respect.

Events, actions, or practices that violate the community's values or sense of propriety undermine confidence. Rumor is an enemy of public confidence. If no action is taken to investigate rumors to see if they are true, they may be publicized through the media or through the grapevine and be blown out of proportion.

One of our bus drivers was arrested for driving while under the influence. That caused quite a ruckus.

A film on human sexuality appropriate for college students was mistakenly shown to a group of high school sophomores. That resulted in a series of local newspaper editorials.

High-confidence districts have built a bank of trust and respect that reduces the chance of blunders or flaws being blown out of proportion. Open lines of communication and willingness to attend to problems help to stem the rumor mill. Clear policies and procedures for dealing with incidents that offend community standards assure the community that the problem is being addressed in a way that is fair to all parties involved. A history of being "up front" with the media about school problems in general will result in fairer and less sensationalized press coverage when a really unusual incident occurs.

Negative publicity causes loss of confidence. The media tend to run stories on school problems rather than successes (a notable exception being coverage of school sports). Also, many newspapers do not have reporters who are well informed about education issues, so their stories do not provide the reader with the background or context for understanding the problems they are writing about. When the media persist in reporting only negative stories, it is bound to have an effect on community confidence in the schools.

> The irresponsible reporting of such things as massed achievement scores and the general public's acceptance of such reports without asking for such things as comparisons based on ability levels has set up a vicious cycle of lowered confidence in public education in general.

> The media seem to publish any negative incidents about the city and are reluctant to be objective in that reporting.

> Critical charges and statements made by representatives of the teachers' association to the media can get too much publicity and cause public anxiety.

> Any bad publicity in regard to discipline will probably hurt the most. A few years ago a parent went to the newspaper with a story about his daughter's purse being stolen. It did happen and can happen anywhere, but the story got headlines and gave readers a bad impression of the school.

High-confidence districts have developed enough trust in their communities so that occasional negative reporting does not arouse undue concern. They also work to "educate" (not to control) media personnel so they will understand more about educational processes, and they provide the media with leads to stories on the good things the schools are doing.

Failure to communicate or communicating equivocally erodes public confidence. Failure to communicate causes suspicion and doubt. Failure to get a straight answer causes one to question the competence of those who are supposed to know.

> Lack of communication or a laissez-faire attitude about communicating with parents can cause loss of confidence. So can an uncaring attitude of teachers toward parents or students. Poor communication between the school administration and its staff also causes problems with confidence. Weak links of communication from administration to staff, students, and community will cause you lots of problems.

> The contradictory information that comes during contract negotiations leaves a community confused; and a confused community is one without confidence.

Lack of openness, dishonesty, or misrepresenting facts to the community and media all make the community doubt everything you say. Ignoring problems can cause the same doubt. Everybody out there sees it. Why can't the people who are supposed to do something about it see it? Whenever problems or concerns are not addressed by the school — whether it is substance abuse or lack of student achievement — you are planting seeds of discontent.

High-confidence districts communicate with their communities frequently and through a number of channels. They also create channels through which their publics communicate back to them. Their communications are marked by honesty, openness, and genuine respect for their publics.

Student achievement that falls short of what parents and the community expect reduces confidence. When a district or school has a tradition of academic achievement and it falls below expected levels, the community becomes uneasy. At the same time, if a district launches an all-out campaign to raise achievement scores and neglects the caring aspects of student/teacher relationships, then confidence can decline.

Poor performance on national standardized tests or declining SAT scores can cost us a lot in this community.

After all the publicity about how bad schools are, this district expects us to increase scores on standardized tests as quickly as possible. But if we aren't particular about how we do it, it may cost us more in the long run than any favorable publicity about improved achievement scores.

Schools and districts with high public confidence give priority to both academic achievement and student welfare. They strive to maintain the achievements that the community has come to expect. In addition, since the mid-1970s, many of these districts have raised their own achievement expectations for learning and, in so doing, have raised the expectations in their communities.

Poor discipline in schools results in loss of confidence. Negative student behavior reflects on the school and arouses public disapproval.

Student discipline problems, especially drug use, will cause the community to withdraw its support and call for your head.

High dropout rates, low achievement scores, vandalism, strikes — these are the things that cause loss in public confidence.

85

We had a high school principal who let discipline go to pot, and we lost the community over that. It had to be cleared up.

You can lose a lot of support over corporal punishment. I don't think most educators know how much that costs all of us. It especially hurts, of course, when a teacher or principal hits kids for some petty thing like chewing gum or not doing homework.

High-confidence schools and districts seem to achieve good discipline through the same processes they use for gaining public confidence. Involvement fosters commitment, which results in responsible participation. (See Phi Delta Kappa Commission on Discipline 1982.)

Complacency can cause a loss of confidence. One of the major challenges facing leaders of good schools is living up to their reputation for "goodness." Being high on a pedestal can lead to overconfidence. It is easy to fall into a pattern of complacency when things seem to be going well.

The issue we may ignore in the coming year is complacency. We were recently recognized as one of the top 104 middle schools in the country by the U.S. Department of Education. I am afraid it might become a new excuse for staff to maintain the status quo. Although I firmly believe we have a good school, I think we could be more creative in the classroom. We let some students fail, and we teach to the group not to the individual. The award mentions our "adaptation to growth," which is justified; but it also mentions "new, creative solutions to teaching," which I do not see. It it not easy to initiate new procedures for helping all students learn when a school has just been told it is the best. Some of our kids will end up losing because of this award if we are not careful. In a community that thrives on the public relations that come with such awards, a principal must keep a sense of proportion.

Whenever the central administration becomes overconfident, what may be overlooked or minimized is the importance of continuing an open discussion with constituencies within and outside of the school system.

Complacency is difficult to overcome in a school district, particularly if it is located in an area where no neighboring districts exceed its achievements or its reputation. High-confidence districts do not become complacent, because they maintain open communications, conduct frequent monitoring, and engage in ongoing improvement efforts. They also employ staff with fresh perspectives, which helps prevent programs from becoming stagnant and prevents vested interests from controlling decision making and practice.

Criticism of schools at the national level can cause a decline in confidence at the local level. While much recent criticism is cast in language that purports to support the public schools, its effect has been to put both effective and ineffective schools on the defensive in many communities (Wayson et al. 1988, pp. 140, 143).

> At the national level, we believe the issuance of several conflicting reports has caused some confusion for the public. The *A Nation at Risk* report did cause a loss of confidence in our schools, even in those that had received national recognition.

> The constant barrage of negative evaluations of schools by the press at national, state, and local levels has undermined public confidence. These reports seldom say that *some* schools are bad, *some* teachers are bad. They seldom give credit to good schools or good teachers.

Negative national publicity has not hurt high-confidence schools too much, although many report having to spend a lot of time and energy to alleviate community concerns stemming from negative publicity (see Wayson et al. 1988, pp. 136, 143; also Rossman et al. 1986). These schools and their communities know that the criticism does not apply to their schools. Indeed, many of these schools and districts are well ahead of national trends; they have already identified problems and have come up with solutions that now serve as models for other districts to emulate.

Making changes without involving all parties who are affected by the changes erodes confidence. School improvements take time, energy, resources, and commitment. Staff must admit to the problem, must accept a role in solving it, and must be able to implement the solutions. When school systems are under public pressure, they often are tempted to do something that is quick and easy or that upsets the staff as little as possible. In their efforts to appease public concern, they fail to involve those directly concerned; and as a result, little or no real change occurs (see Wayson et al. 1988, Chapter Two).

> The greatest loss of confidence came years ago when I failed to communicate adequately with the staff about what we meant with a program of "Individualized Instruction" in the classrooms. It was threatening, and it almost ruined me and the staff. The

teachers who were threatened most already understood and practiced individualized instruction with their pupils. We finally communicated, and they came to see that they did not have to work out a completely individual program for each student in order to meet individual needs.

Years ago we opened the first open-space school in the system. Neither staff nor the community were prepared for it. After much frustration during the first year, which almost destroyed the school, the staff and the community began to believe in themselves and the program. Building this confidence has required energy, patience, and time.

High-confidence schools view change as a systemic effort. They involve people from all levels in planning and implementing change. They go beyond superficial inservice and offer extensive staff development programs that achieve genuine understanding and commitment from those who have to carry out the change. They keep their communities fully informed and frequently teach parents and others about the proposed innovations.

Failure to adapt to demographic changes in the community results in loss of confidence. Whether the new population is of higher or lower status, changing populations can create instability among school personnel. Familiar routines no longer work, and the staff loses its own sense of efficacy. Frequently, the staff blames its uneasiness on the new student population; "war stories" start to circulate as a form of protection for the institutional "ego." Unfamiliarity with the new student population leads to prejudice. Lack of skill in communicating with these new students and their parents leads to increasing discipline problems and lower achievement. All of these forces combine to reduce public confidence, and efforts to solve the problem are made difficult because the true nature of the problem is seldom recognized.

Our district has been known for its wealth. We have had high achievers to work with, and instruction has been geared to them. Now, there are many apartments where there once were horse farms. Rental housing is now available for families who formerly could not afford to live in the area. Some are fleeing from desegregation in the city, so they stretch their budget to come to our school. The new students do not have the background and advantages our former students had, and their achievement is lower than some of the staff is used to. Teachers who were

comfortable teaching high-achieving students now find it difficult to reach those who are not yet achievers. We are already
hearing terminology such as "low-ability students" and "untal-
ented kids" instead of "kids whose talents have not yet been developed." Our achievement scores will drop until we realize that
complaining about the differences will not help, but adjusting
to them will.

High-confidence districts are aware of demographic changes and
anticipate the impact they will have on their schools. They engage
in staff development programs to create curriculum and instructional approaches that are appropriate for a changing student population.
They make special efforts to establish a welcoming and caring climate for these new populations. Administrative policies are directed
toward educating these new students rather than a "circle the wagons"
attitude to protect what once was.

Racial conflict causes loss of confidence. Community conflict in-
tensifies when the issues are race-related. Demands for changes by
blacks are perceived as threats. Even enlightened citizens express
doubt about the outcomes of race-related issues.

> Continuous racial and ethnic conflict and strife causes peo-
> ple to think that achievement will drop, that discipline will go
> to hell, and that the schools are unsafe for their kids.

High-confidence districts are sensitive to racial issues. They train
staff to relate to people from different racial backgrounds. By going
into the community for home visits and other activities, the staff earns
trust from the black community. By demonstrating concern for all
students and by treating them and their parents with respect, the district helps to unite the community on educational matters. Because
these districts have established a reputation for fairness, when a racial incident occurs it does not escalate into a major conflict. In many
instances these districts have been instrumental in improving race
relations in other areas of community life.

Resistance to court-ordered desegregation causes loss of confidence.
Desegregation orders by the courts are often perceived as some "outside" source telling the community what to do. Resistance to these
orders often involves protracted litigation accompanied by vitriolic
accusations. Implementation is delayed or purposely flawed to prove
that the "outsider" is wrong or that solutions will not work. Such actions create instability in the schools and turn public sentiment against
the decision — all of which is quite destructive to public confidence.

89

Desegregation and busing is a cause for loss of confidence. People have all those feelings about blacks just not being part of good schools. It may be unfair, but that's the way it comes out more often than not. It is the first question the real estate people ask, and they don't help matters any.

The board members and even some of the school officials kept saying that the schools would be harmed. What was the public to believe? Then they undermined the staff development program and kept moving the staff around willy-nilly, making all the teachers mad. Then they kept repeating to the press that people were moving out of the city in droves. After the big day came, the bus service was awful because of poor management; people began to suspend kids for just about anything. And the buses and the blacks got blamed for it all. It straightened out, and we got a new board and a new superintendent; but we still don't have the confidence we once had.

A nearby metropolitan school district's desegregation case has drawn much negative press, and a lot of people are worried about whether their kids will learn in the schools there.

Because most of the districts in our survey had already undergone desegregation, they did not report what they had done prior to desegregation to maintain public confidence. However, after desegregation they reported that with new school boards and changes in administration there was commitment to educate children no matter how they came to school or what their ethnic background was. New public confidence came by involving all segments of the community in planning and problem-solving, by opening schools to more parent and community participation, and by training staff members to relate to minority children and their families.

Failure to provide equal educational opportunity causes loss of confidence among minority groups. Minority groups are not always minorities in a school district or on the governing bodies that control the schools. Any evidence that minority students are not getting equal educational opportunites can cause serious erosions of confidence among minority members in the community.

Public confidence suffered once here when we had some officials who just didn't understand some sensitive religious policy issues.

Whether the minority is religious, racial, or linguistic, high-confidence districts recognize that they must be sensitive to minori-

90

ty groups if they expect to have their confidence. Schools and districts in our survey seem to have learned this from the conflicts in the 1960s and 1970s. Much of the confidence they now enjoy from all segments of the community seems to have come from their realization of the ideals of American democratic education.

Summary

Conflict is inevitable is schools and communities. How school leaders handle conflict determines whether there is a loss of public confidence. Leaders in high-confidence schools and districts are skillful in managing conflict. They operate on a daily basis in ways that "bank" confidence, which they can draw on when controversy erupts. They do it by educating, informing, involving, and problem solving rather than by controlling, evading, denying, or glossing over problems.

These school districts gained the confidence of their communities by selecting quality personnel and giving them the autonomy to design programs that would achieve the districts' goals. They stressed honesty and openness in their interactions with the public. They had high levels of involvement from parents and other community members on district committees or task forces. They recruited great numbers of volunteers to perform important functions in the schools. They communicated frequently with the community and had both formal and informal ways of assessing public opinion and concerns about the school. They responded to identified problems in a non-defensive manner and took steps to solve those problems if they could be solved. They demonstrated that they cared about students' welfare and their learning by offering diverse programs to meet a variety of needs and interests.

Chapter Nine
A Checklist for Developing Public Confidence

From the reports of schools and districts in our survey, we learned much about high-confidence institutions. In this final chapter we present a compilation of their major features in the form of three checklists, which may be used as the basis for staff planning. These lists are not exhaustive, nor is it possible to identify any single characteristic as the determining factor in creating schools with high confidence. No doubt a complex interaction of a number of factors contributes to high levels of confidence.

The first checklist covers factors in the school or district settings; the second deals with attitudes and values that permeate the school or district; the third presents specific activities carried out by the schools or districts. A school staff or others can use these checklists to compare their own schools or districts with those that have high levels of confidence. It is not necessary for a school to exhibit all the characteristics; in fact, no school in our sample did so. But by using the checklists, staff and students can identify some areas they could develop further. This kind of self-assessment identifies organizational strengths and weaknesses as perceived by its members and provides a basis for future planning.

Checklist I: Character of the Setting

For each statement, indicate the degree to which the statement is characteristic of your school or school district by circling the appropriate number from "1" (the statement is not at all true of my school or district) to "5" (the statement is always true of my school or district).

A. Students

1 2 3 4 5   1. Students are high achievers in academic areas as evidenced by number of Merit Scholarship winners, high SAT scores, and other high achievement test scores.

1 2 3 4 5   2. Students are high achievers in non-academic activities such as sports, debate, publications, music, and drama.

1 2 3 4 5   3. Students represent the school well in settings outside the school.

1 2 3 4 5   4. Students exhibit pride in the school; they wear school insignia or talk about the school with pride.

1 2 3 4 5   5. Students from different socioeconomic and ethnic backgrounds mix and work well together.

1 2 3 4 5   6. A large proportion of students are accepted into colleges.

1 2 3 4 5   7. The student population is made up of diverse socioeconomic and ethnic groups.

1 2 3 4 5   8. Students are engaged in productive activities at school.

1 2 3 4 5   9. Few students drop out.

1 2 3 4 5   10. Student attendance is high.

B. School Staff

1 2 3 4 5   1. Teachers are knowledgeable and well prepared in the fields they teach.

1 2 3 4 5   2. Teachers are skilled in teaching their subject matter to students.

1 2 3 4 5   3. Most teachers have graduate degrees in their fields.

1 2 3 4 5   4. Staff members represent the school well by their demeanor and dress.

1 2 3 4 5   5. Staff members have high morale.

1 2 3 4 5   6. Administrators and teachers are not defensive when the public expresses concern about some aspect of the school.

1 2 3 4 5   7. Administrators and other staff want to find out how the public views the school.

1 2 3 4 5   8. Staff members are helpful to parents and other visitors to the school.

1 2 3 4 5   9. Staff turnover is minimal.

1 2 3 4 5 10. Staff members treat students as they want their own children to be treated.

1 2 3 4 5 11. Staff members care about students.

1 2 3 4 5 12. The superintendent sees that school personnel get the help they need to solve problems.

1 2 3 4 5 13. Staff attendance is high.

C. Curriculum

1 2 3 4 5   1. The curriculum is varied with many options for students in foreign language, science, mathematics, and literature.

1 2 3 4 5   2. The curriculum serves students of varied ability: the gifted, the developmentally disabled, and those with special talents and interests.

1 2 3 4 5   3. The secondary curriculum includes courses to help students in basic skills of reading and mathematics.

1 2 3 4 5   4. The program of studies is structured and demanding.

1 2 3 4 5   5. The curriculum is developed through cooperative planning by staff, parents, and administrators.

D. Extracurricular Activities

1 2 3 4 5   1. Extracurricular activities are rich and varied.

1 2 3 4 5   2. All students who wish to do so have an opportunity to participate in extracurricular activities.

1 2 3 4 5   3. Participation in extracurricular activities is high; 70% to 90% of students participate.

1 2 3 4 5   4. Staff support for extracurricular activities is high.

E. School Climate

1 2 3 4 5   1. The school is open to parents and the public.

1 2 3 4 5   2. Goals for school improvement are shared by staff, students, parents, and administration.

1 2 3 4 5   3. The lack of litter and graffiti reflect pride in the building and grounds.

1 2 3 4 5   4. The building is attractive and welcoming to guests.

1 2 3 4 5   5. The building provides space for special activities, such as practice rooms for student musicians and an auditorium for musical and theater productions.

1 2 3 4 5   6. The school and district is honest and open when dealing with the public about problems.

Checklist II: Attitudes and Values

A. Students

1 2 3 4 5   1. Students feel that the school is theirs and that they belong there.

1 2 3 4 5   2. Students are proud of being part of the school.

1 2 3 4 5   3. Students enjoy being in the school.

1 2 3 4 5   4. Student cooperation is evident in such activities as orienting new students and peer tutoring.

B. School Staff

1 2 3 4 5   1. Staff members believe every child can learn.

1 2 3 4 5   2. Staff members are happy to be working in the school.

1 2 3 4 5   3. Staff members show pride in the school.

1 2 3 4 5   4. Staff members trust students.

1 2 3 4 5   5. Staff members are positive about students and praise them for good performance.

1 2 3 4 5   6. Staff members regard everything done in the school as being for the benefit of students.

1 2 3 4 5   7. The staff exhibit a high degree of professional responsibility.

C. School Climate

1 2 3 4 5   1. The school visibly values and supports learning.

1 2 3 4 5   2. Pride in the school is demonstrated on a daily basis.

1 2 3 4 5   3. The school is a warm and welcoming place.

1 2 3 4 5   4. Students and staff value positive behaviors; one hears no booing at sporting events.

1 2 3 4 5   5. Honesty is valued; problems are openly discussed and examined.

1 2 3 4 5   6. Students are trusted to use good judgment and are expected to practice self-discipline.

Checklist III: Activities and Programs for Developing Public Confidence

A. Students

1 2 3 4 5 1. Student advisement is individualized and continuous; for example, every adult in the school has a set of advisees whom they keep for several years.

1 2 3 4 5 2. Programs are available to encourage students to support and help one another; for example, peer tutoring.

1 2 3 4 5 3. Academic progress is checked frequently and followed by help if needed; for example, teachers may get computerized printouts of students who are falling behind in work.

1 2 3 4 5 4. All staff members, including coaches, club sponsors, counselors, administrators, and others, assist classroom teachers in motivating students to perform to the best of their ability.

1 2 3 4 5 5. Work is individualized to ensure student success.

1 2 3 4 5 6. Student achievements are recognized and celebrated; for example, through awards assemblies, certificates, and announcements in local media.

1 2 3 4 5 7. Programs are available for students who need or want to spend more time at the school; for example, one "early bird" program includes courses in karate, bridge, music, and dance.

1 2 3 4 5 8. Special programs are available to orient new students; for example, assemblies, student guides, or a two-week "camp" in late summer before school starts.

1 2 3 4 5 9. Programs are available to support students with special social problems; for example, pregnant teenagers receive training in parenting and are provided day-care facilities after their babies are born.

1 2 3 4 5 10. Students are rewarded for maintaining good discipline; for example, longer lunch hours or a movie are sometimes used as rewards.

B. Personnel Policies and Staff Development

1 2 3 4 5 1. Teachers visit other classes or other schools to get ideas and give feedback.

1 2 3 4 5   2. Teachers receive compliments when a job is well done.

1 2 3 4 5   3. Staff development is considered important enough that adequate time is provided for it.

1 2 3 4 5   4. Teachers plan their own staff development.

1 2 3 4 5   5. Teachers have a role in developing a staff evaluation system that is objective and fair.

1 2 3 4 5   6. Care is taken to select teachers who are committed to attaining the school's mission.

1 2 3 4 5   7. The staff meets regularly to discuss problems and to collaborate on planning.

1 2 3 4 5   8. Administrators visit staff members who have personal crises; for example, illness or death in the family.

1 2 3 4 5   9. Staff members enjoy social activities together; for example, breakfasts, potlucks, or trips together.

1 2 3 4 5 10. Staff committees establish guidelines for spending staff development funds.

1 2 3 4 5 11. Staff development focuses on the resolution of real problems in the school; for example, if map skills in the fifth grade are weak, then they become the focus for staff development training.

C. Governance and Management

1 2 3 4 5   1. Students are actively involved in setting policies and procedures for the school; for example, students participate in advisory groups on discipline policies.

1 2 3 4 5   2. Student leaders take responsible roles in managing extracurricular activities; for example, assemblies, dances, student senate meetings, and clubs.

1 2 3 4 5   3. Student leaders take responsible roles in managing certain school business functions; for example, cafeteria money and attendance.

1 2 3 4 5   4. Student governance groups make important decisions; for example, they control their own funds.

1 2 3 4 5   5. Parent advisory councils participate in school evaluation and offer input on curricular and extracurricular offerings.

1 2 3 4 5   6. Expectations for proper behavior are clearly stated in a code of conduct.

1 2 3 4 5   7. Discipline practices are equitable.

1 2 3 4 5   8. School officials use alternatives to suspensions and corporal punishment for violations of school rules; for example, in-school suspension or Saturday school in which students participate in useful learning activities.

1 2 3 4 5   9. The superintendent (or principal) has an advisory council, made up of staff and community members, which meets regularly.

1 2 3 4 5   10. Parents are encouraged to express their concerns about the school or district; a forum is provided where they can do this.

1 2 3 4 5   11. All staff participate in making and implementing plans to improve school policies in discipline and other areas.

D. Curriculum and Instruction

1 2 3 4 5   1. The curriculum provides opportunities for students to extend and apply their knowledge; for example, field trips, laboratory work, and internships in industry.

1 2 3 4 5   2. The curriculum encourages students to conduct research; for example, studying insect life found on the playground or conducting opinion polls on a controversial issue.

1 2 3 4 5   3. Special education students are properly diagnosed and are placed in the least restrictive learning environment.

1 2 3 4 5   4. Students are given an opportunity to show what they have learned; for example, "Young Authors" programs, art shows, or recitals.

1 2 3 4 5   5. Special programs showcase the academic talents of students in all curriculum areas; for example, Academic Olympiads, math competitions, creative writing publications, and science fairs.

1 2 3 4 5   6. Audiovisuals and education technology are used to vary and enliven instruction; for example, overhead projectors, videotapes, films, and computers.

1 2 3 4 5   7. Various instructional methods are used; for example, discussion, debate, mediated lectures, outside speakers, projects, field trips, or original inquiry.

1 2 3 4 5   8. Work experience programs provide adolescents an opportunity to explore careers and become familiar with the world of work.

1 2 3 4 5   9. Special skills programs are available to students who have difficulty but who are not classified as special education students; for example, writing clinics, math tutorials, or assertiveness training.

1 2 3 4 5   10. Students' creative work is published and disseminated to parents and a wider audience; for example, student-produced books, videotapes, and radio programs.

1 2 3 4 5   11. Students are encouraged to do concentrated study in areas of interest to them; scheduling is flexible enough to accommodate in-depth study of topics.

1 2 3 4 5   12. Both students and staff can articulate what the school's goals are.

E. Extracurricular Activities

1 2 3 4 5   1. Enough extracurricular activities are available for every student to participate and perform leadership roles.

1 2 3 4 5   2. Extracurricular activities are varied enough to meet a range of student interests.

1 2 3 4 5   3. A large proportion of students participate in extracurricular activities.

1 2 3 4 5   4. Regular courses are supplemented with activities in which students can apply what they have learned; for example, home economics courses include catering in the cafeteria.

1 2 3 4 5   5. Students have opportunities to engage in significant out-of-school projects; for example, one school raised more than $6,000 by sellng Christmas trees, which they had grown over a five-year period.

1 2 3 4 5   6. Students participate in clean-up and school beautification projects.

1 2 3 4 5   7. Students have opportunities to perform significant services that are educational in nature; for example, students help in a day-care center that serves staff and students.

F. Communications: Internal and External

1 2 3 4 5   1. School and PTA newsletters go out regularly to parents and others.

1 2 3 4 5   2. Interim reports are provided for students who are not making good progress or are failing.

1 2 3 4 5   3. Students publish a school newspaper.

1 2 3 4 5   4. Staff members make frequent personal contacts with parents; for example, by telephone, letters, home visits, or conferences.

1 2 3 4 5   5. Staff members make a conscious effort to speak positively about the school and its students when they interact with community members.

1 2 3 4 5   6. Students project a positive image of the school when they talk with members of the community.

1 2 3 4 5   7. The school or district has established close ties with local newspapers and other news media.

1 2 3 4 5   8. An informative district newsletter is disseminated to all employees.

1 2 3 4 5   9. The school or district promotes contact between parents; for example, one district publishes names and telephone numbers of parents who are willing to provide information to others; others have neighborhood meetings.

1 2 3 4 5 10. An attractive, informative school handbook goes to all students and parents.

1 2 3 4 5 11. Parents receive prompt communication about student absences.

1 2 3 4 5 12. School goals are written in plain English so they are understandable to parents from the beginning.

1 2 3 4 5 13. Readable, positively phrased (bilingual, if necessary) publications concerning school goals, policies, and programs are available from the school and district offices.

1 2 3 4 5 14. Children's work is displayed at various places in the community.

1 2 3 4 5 15. An "open door" policy invites the public to visit schools or attend school meetings at any time.

1 2 3 4 5 16. The principal (or other staff members) meets regularly with community groups to learn about their concerns.

G. Buildings and Grounds

1 2 3 4 5   1. Students and staff work to keep the building clean, attractive, and free of litter and graffiti.

1 2 3 4 5   2. Student artwork is displayed in all areas of the building.
1 2 3 4 5   3. The building space is used for a variety of learning activities.
1 2 3 4 5   4. Periodic surveys are made of the physical facility to see if it reflects the goals of the school.
1 2 3 4 5   5. Students are actively involved in managing and making decisions about physical facilities; for example, they might manage the cafeteria and have a vote on the color of paint used or on landscaping.

H. Parents and Community

1 2 3 4 5   1. Parent advisory groups meet regularly.
1 2 3 4 5   2. Parent representatives are invited to attend the principal's council and the superintendent's advisory council.
1 2 3 4 5   3. Accurate and up-to-date information is readily available to people who call and want to know more about the district.
1 2 3 4 5   4. Students perform volunteer services in the community; for example, entertaining patients at nursing homes and hospitals or working for community agencies.
1 2 3 4 5   5. The community is able to use the school for adult education and recreation.
1 2 3 4 5   6. School programs, in addition to sports events, attract high attendance.
1 2 3 4 5   7. Community resources are used to enrich the curriculum; for example, professors from local colleges and other community members with special expertise teach courses or serve as guest speakers in classes.
1 2 3 4 5   8. Students are provided career information from people working in a variety of occupations.
1 2 3 4 5   9. The school uses external programs to extend students' learning; for example, Outward Bound or the local community theater group.
1 2 3 4 5 10. Students participate in local businesses through work/study programs, internships, or mentor programs.
1 2 3 4 5 11. Community "booster" groups support music, drama and other student activities in addition to athletics.

1 2 3 4 5 12. Parents or members of school-associated groups gather information from the community as input for decision making.

1 2 3 4 5 13. The school provides real estate agencies with information about the schools.

1 2 3 4 5 14. Student representatives attend meetings of community agencies.

1 2 3 4 5 15. Staff members are actively involved in community affairs and volunteer to work in community agencies.

1 2 3 4 5 16. Students provide services to the community; for example, Special Olympics, clean-up campaigns, or adopt-a-grandparent programs.

1 2 3 4 5 17. Community organizations honor students for their accomplishments.

1 2 3 4 5 18. Parent and community opinion is polled on a regular basis.

1 2 3 4 5 19. Schools provide programs that have become community traditions; for example, a 200-voice choir and a popular teen arts festival.

1 2 3 4 5 20. Community members participate in long-term evaluation projects; for example, a committee on "excellence" may conduct a study for a year or more.

1 2 3 4 5 21. A large number of parent volunteers fill a variety of roles.

1 2 3 4 5 22. The school has a special training program for parent volunteers on how to help students.

1 2 3 4 5 23. Community leadership conferences are sponsored by the school or district.

1 2 3 4 5 24. School board meetings are open to the community.

1 2 3 4 5 25. A comprehensive community education program brings in people who would not ordinarily visit the school.

1 2 3 4 5 26. Achievement test scores are regularly published to inform the public about how the schools are doing.

1 2 3 4 5 27. Administrators and faculty live in the attendance area of their schools.

I. Finance

1 2 3 4 5   1. The school district demonstrates sound fiscal management.

1 2 3 4 5   2. Parents raise funds for special events and activities; for example, parents have "phonathons" to raise scholarship money.

1 2 3 4 5   3. An active alumni association helps to generate funds for the school or district.

1 2 3 4 5   4. Business representatives advise the district on financial management.

1 2 3 4 5   5. Regular reports inform citizens about the financial status of the district.

1 2 3 4 5   6. Teachers' salaries are competitive with surrounding districts.

1 2 3 4 5   7. The superintendent has a community advisory council, which meets regularly to review budget matters.

1 2 3 4 5   8. The district has a foundation for raising and disbursing funds for worthy projects not funded under the regular budget.

Using These Checklists

These checklists were not designed to be used as research instruments. Rather, they are intended to serve as a stimulus for collaborative problem solving, which seems to be a hallmark of high-confidence schools. The various items on the checklists provide starting points for school staff and community members when undertaking efforts to improve public confidence.

Below is a description of a process for using the checklists, which has been tested with a number of school staffs engaged in school improvement programs.* The chief strength of the process is that it enables a group to develop a clear sense of purpose from which come guidelines for action.

The process can take place in short sessions, such as team or faculty meetings, but preferably a group should take at least one full day to work through the process. An ideal arrangement is a weekend re-

---

*We acknowledge work done in the Department of Educational Policy and Leadership at Ohio State University by Gay Su Pinnell, George Wynn, Cynthia Jackson, Theodis Fipps, and Pamela Ptaszek and by the staffs at Mooney, Hart, and Herrick Schools in Cleveland, and Mifflin, Buckeye, Crestview, Brookhaven, and Mohawk Schools in Columbus, who in 1980-82 helped to develop this process.

treat setting in a remote area. Some schools have funded such retreats, or they negotiate with a social agency, church, or business to use their facilities at minimal cost to the school. The facilities used should be able to provide comfortable seating around small tables. The only materials needed are sheets of chart paper, masking tape, and felt-tip markers.

The process can be adapted for use by elementary or secondary school staffs, including community members. All participants should read Chapter Seven of this handbook prior to the first session. Also, the process is expedited if participants have filled out the checklists prior to the meeting. This allows the facilitator or another member of the group to tabulate the results and have them available at the beginning of the meeting.

Step One. Organize the participants into work groups of no more than five people. In making up the groups, strive for a mix of grade levels, subject specialists, administrators, parents, and community members in each group. This deliberate mixing of work groups provides for greater diversity of ideas during Step Three, the brainstorming session. Allow some time for members in each group to get to know one another.

Step Two. The facilitator can preselect a small list of activities from the checklists if they have been completed and tabulated ahead of time. If time permits, each group can select a small list of activities from the checklists that it would like to implement. Whatever selection procedure is used, the activities selected to work on would be those that had received the lowest ratings on the five-point scale. Also, groups may add activities not on the checklist that they think need attention in the school. Have each group list the selected activities on chart paper and post them on a wall, so that the list of activities is in constant view as the groups engage in the process.

Step Three. Instruct the small groups to focus their attention on one activity listed on the chart paper and then brainstorm ideas using the following question: "If we are making progress toward implementing this activity, what will we be able to see, hear, taste, smell, or touch in this building three months (or some other date in the future) from now?" Any idea suggested is listed on chart paper. All ideas are accepted; no one may comment on, criticize, or make fun of any idea that is proposed. Give the groups about five minutes to brainstorm. For each activity that is brainstormed will come some clear and tangible actions for implementing the activity.

Step Four. Have each small group hang its charts with the activity and brainstorming ideas so they are in clear view of the whole assembly. Give participants time to review all the chart sheets. Invite participants to ask questions if clarification is needed about any of the brainstorming ideas. The originators of the ideas can then explain what they meant.

Step Five. If necessary, a second round of brainstorming can take place at this point if the actions proposed to accomplish the activity on the lists are still vague or too general. For example, if the selected activity is "Teachers plan their own staff development" and the brainstormed action is "Staff development programs will be interesting," this may be too vague and intangible. When this occurs, ask the group to do some more brainstorming by rephrasing the original question as follows: "What will we see, hear, taste, smell, or touch in this school three months from now if staff development programs are more interesting?" Usually, this will result in more detailed suggestions that can lead to specific actions.

Step Six. In this session the whole group makes its choices about where it wants to put its energy. Participants review all of the action ideas listed on the charts and decide on a few to which everyone in the group will commit themselves and agree to contribute all they possibly can to making them work. Participants are not to vote but are to engage in as much discussion as necessary to clarify, to adapt, or to eliminate actions, so that the final list is one that all participants can understand, accept, and pledge to make happen.

In this session, any member of the group may stand firm on any action that he or she feels is important. Anyone may propose eliminating an action that seems trivial or unimportant. However, it is incumbent on all members to use persuasion and rational argument to convince others to join them on a decision. The process is compromised if logrolling, bargaining, or power tactics are used to get a decision on a specific action. The final list must be at least reasonably acceptable to all participants. Although Step Six is presented here as a whole-group activity, it can be conducted in two parts: first as a small-group activity and then as a whole-group activity. This allows for more involvement and prevents dominant personalities from exerting too much influence, which sometimes happens in large groups.

Step Seven. When the final list of actions to be taken has been written on a sheet of chart paper, each member of the group signs his or her name on the sheet. This symbolic act signifies that the participants understand the actions to be taken and agree to work to achieve them.

The seven-step process described above takes time, but it is time well spent. It requires participants to listen to one another, to discuss, and even to argue until they reach consensus. The outcome is a list of cooperatively determined objectives that the group has committed itself to support. This is a beginning.

Of course, no list ever ensures success (which is why school board philosophy statements or lists of goals have never improved a school). Someone must provide leadership *after* the list of actions is selected. Such leadership usually becomes the responsibility of the school staff, who will have to develop a plan for implementing the actions. Procedures for group planning may be found in Chapter 5 of *Handbook for Developing Schools With Good Discipline* (Phi Delta Kappa Commission on Discipline 1982); also in Schmuck and Runkel (1985); Feldman (1985); Vaill (1971); and Howard, Howell, and Brainard (1987).

Everything possible must be done to show that the list of actions for school improvement is not just another list. It should appear a number of times in a number of places for staff, parents, and students to see and to refer to. The list should be used to guide decisions in staff meetings, and it should be referred to frequently when evaluating progress. The list should be a topic of conversation as much in the faculty lounge as in formal meetings. In short, the list should be taken seriously.

A Final Word

It is not clear which individual factors are most important for gaining public confidence. What is clear is that no one factor, by itself, can raise confidence. High-confidence schools in our sample used different combinations of the activities appearing on the checklists; no school used all of them. Most of the schools were like Taft Middle School in Albuquerque, New Mexico:

> Taft did not receive recognition for its building's varied use, its balanced ethnic community, its "Side-by-Side" program, its cooperation among kids of different social levels, its innovative cafeteria plan, its interest in computer literacy, its varied outside classroom clubs and activities, its excellent staff, its good

administrative leadership, or its parent involvement. Recognition was received because of all those features *and more*.

Just what is the "more" is not clear. However, our hunch is that it is the dynamics of a committed and able school staff working together to solve whatever problems prevent them from attaining the educational outcomes they want to achieve. Schools that have some combination of the programs and practices associated with the high-confidence schools described in this book have a high probability of enjoying high public confidence. Their continuing challenge is to maintain that confidence.

References and Recommended Readings

"A + Schools: Portraits of Schools that Work." *Instructor and Teacher* 94 (September 1984): 20-22; 95 (September 1985): 22-23; 95 (November 1985): 18-21; 95 (February 1986): 26-28; 95 (March 1986): 26-28; 95 (April 1986): 24-26; 96 (October 1986): 22-25. Each month, *Instructor and Teacher* features a school. Those listed here were included in this study.

Achilles, Charles M., and Lintz, M. Nan. "Information and Communication: Tools for Increasing Confidence in the Schools." Paper presented at the American Educational Research Association, New Orleans, 1984. ERIC No. Ed 244-373

Achilles, Charles M., and Lintz, M. Nan. "Public Confidence in Public Education: A Growing Concern in the 80's." Paper presented at the Mid-South Educational Research Association, 1983. ERIC No. Ed 242-034

Achilles, Charles M.; Lintz, M. Nan; and Wayson, William W. "Building Public Confidence in Public Education: Some Preliminary Data." *Tennessee Education* 14 (Spring 1984): 14-19.

Achilles, Charles M.; Lintz, M. Nan; and Wayson, William W. "Confidence Building Strategies in the Public Schools." *Planning and Change* 16 (Summer 1985): 85-95.

Andrew, Loyd D.; Parks, David J.; Nelson, Lynda A.; and the Phi Delta Kappa Commission on Teacher/Faculty Morale. *Administrator's Handbook for Improving Faculty Morale*. Bloomington, Ind.: Phi Delta Kappa, 1985.

Alexander, Lamar. *"Time for Results*: An Overview." *Phi Delta Kappan* 68 (November 1986): 202-204.

American Association of School Administrators. "Problem Areas for School Administrators." *School Administrator* 40 (July-August 1983): 30.

Armistead, Lew. *Building Confidence in Education*. Reston, Va.: National Association of Secondary School Principals, 1982.

Association for Supervision and Curriculum Development. "Toward More Effective Schools." *Educational Leadership* 40 (December 1982).

Astuto, Terry A., and Clark, David L. "Strength of Organizational Coupling in the Instructionally Effective School." *Urban Education* 19 (January 1985): 331-56.

Back, J. "The Effective Schools Concept: An Effective Way to Help Schools Make a Difference." *Education* 105 (Spring 1985): 232-35.

Bagin, Don; Ferguson, Donald; and Marx, Gary. *Public Relations for Administrators*. Arlington. Va.: American Association of School Administrators, 1986.

Bagin, Don; Grazian, F.; and Harrison, C.H. *School Communications: Ideas That Work*. Woodstown, N.J.: Communicaid, 1972.

Banach, William. "How to 'Parent-Proof' A School." *Education Digest* 46 (December 1980): 36-37. Condensed from *Illinois School Board Journal* 48 (July-August 1980): 24.

Bell, Terrel H. "Building Partnerships for Quality Education in Rural America." *American Education* 20 (October 1984): 4-5, 11.

Bell, Terrel H. "Education Policy Development in the Reagan Administration." *Phi Delta Kappan* 67 (March 1986): 487-93.

Bell, Terrel H. *The Thirteenth Man: A Reagan Cabinet Memoir*. Boston: Free Press, 1988.

Berman, Paul, and McLaughlin, Milbray. *Federal Programs Supporting Educational Change, Volume III: Implementing and Sustaining Innovations*. Santa Monica, Calif.: Rand Corporation, 1978.

Biros, Janice. "The Use of Marketing Activities in K-12 Public Schools in New York State." Doctoral dissertation, State University of New York at Albany, 1983.

Blase, Joseph J. "Dimensions of Effective School Leadership: The Teacher's Perspective." *American Educational Research Journal* 24 (Winter 1987): 589-610.

Boyer, Ernest. *High School: A Report on Secondary Education in America*. New York: Harper & Row, 1983.

Boyer, Richard, and Savageau, David. *Places Rated Almanac: Your Guide to Finding the Best Places to Live in America*. Chicago: Rand McNally, 1985.

Bridge, R. Gary, and Blackman, Julie. *A Study of Alternatives in American Education, Vol. IV: Family Choice in Schooling*. Prepared for the National Institute of Education. Santa Monica, Calif.: Rand Corporation, April 1978.

Brooks, Johney. "Marketing the Public School." *Educational Leadership* 40 (October 1982): 22-24.

Bugher, Wilmer. *Polling Attitudes of Community on Education (PACE)*. Bloomington, Ind.: Phi Delta Kappa, 1980.

Burnett, R.D. "Bringing Excellence to a Troubled School." *Vocational Education* 59 (1984): 39-41.

Butterfield, John. "Worthington Schools: Excellence Comes First." *Columbus Monthly* 12 (May 1986): 13-19.

Calabrese, Raymond L., and Anderson, R.E. "The Public School: A Source of Stress and Alienation Among Female Teachers." *Urban Education* 21 (April 1986): 30-41.

Calabrese, Raymond L., and Seldin, Clement A. "A Contextual Analysis of Alienation Among School Constituencies." *Urban Education* 22 (July 1987): 227-37.

Campbell, E.; Faires, C.; and Martin, O. "School Discipline: Policy, Procedures and Potential Discrimination. A Study of Disproportionate Representation of Minority Pupils in School Suspension." *Resources in Education*. ERIC No. ED 227 544, 1 EA 015 438.

Carnegie Forum on Education and the Economy. *A Nation Prepared: Teachers for the 21st Century*. Washington, D.C., 1986.

Carol, Lila N., and Cunningham, Luvern L. "Views of Public Confidence in Education." *Issues in Education* 2 (Fall 1984): 110-26.

Carr, Harold L. "We Integrate the Academics." *Vocational Education* 59 (March 1984): 34-36.

Cattermole, Juleen, and Robinson, Norman. "Effective Home/School Communication: From the Parents' Perspective." *Phi Delta Kappan* 67 (September 1985): 48-50.

Clark, David L. "High School Seniors React to Their Teachers and Their Schools." *Phi Delta Kappan* 68 (March 1987): 503-509.

Clark, Terry A., and McCarthy, Dennis P. "School Improvement in New York City: The Evolution of a Project." *Educational Researcher* 12 (April 1983): 17-24.

Comer, James P. "Parent Participation in the Schools." *Phi Delta Kappan* 67 (February 1986): 442-46.

Corbett, H. Dickson, and D'Amico, Joseph J. "No More Heroes: Creating Systems to Support Change." *Educational Leadership* 44 (September 1986): 70-72.

Corcoran, Thomas B., and Wilson, Bruce L. *The Search for Successful Secondary Schools: The First Three Years of the Secondary School Recognition Program*. Philadelphia: Research for Better Schools, 1986.

Cottrell, Leonard S. "The Competent Community." in *New Perspectives on the American Community*, edited by Roland L. Warren. Chicago: Rand McNally, 1977.

110

Criscuolo, Nicholas P. "A Little PR Goes a Long Way." *Principal* 40 (January 1985): 32-34.

Cuban, Larry. "Transforming the Frog into a Prince: Effective Schools Research, Policy, and Practice at the District Level." *Harvard Educational Review* 54 (1983): 129-51.

Cuban, Larry. "Effective Schools: A Friendly but Cautionary Note." *Phi Delta Kappan* 64 (June 1983): 695-96.

Cunningham, Luvern; and Dunn, Van Bogard. "Interprofessional Policy Analysis: An Aid to Public Policy Formation." *Theory Into Practice* 26 (Spring 1987): 129-33.

Cunningham, Luvern. "Applying Lasswell's Concept in Field Situations: Diagnostic and Prescriptive Values." *Education Administration Quarterly* 17 (Spring 1981): 21-43.

Danzberger, Jacqueline P.; Carol, Lila N.; Cunningham, Luvern L.; Kirst, Michael W.; McCloud, Barbara A.; and Usdan, Michael D. "School Boards: The Forgotten Players on the Educational Team." *Phi Delta Kappan* 69 (September 1987): 53-59.

Danzberger, Jacqueline P., and Usdan, Michael D. "Building Partnerships: The Atlanta Experience." *Phi Delta Kappan* 65 (February 1984): 393-96.

Davis, S. John, and Shingleton, Callie P. "Model High School Provides Answers in Meeting Needs of Education in State." *NASSP Bulletin* 70 (March 1986): 93-99.

Donohue, John W. "One School's Secret." *America* 148 (2 April 1983): 254-58.

Duttweiler, Patricia C. "A Practical School-Based Method for Improving the School Learning Climate." *Education Research Service Spectrum* 4 (1986): 18-21.

Education Research Service. *Needs Assessment of AASA Members, 1983-84: Summary of Responses to a Survey of AASA Members*. Arlington, Va., February 1984.

Elam, Stanley M. "The Gallup Education Surveys: Impressions of a Poll Watcher." *Phi Delta Kappan* 65 (September 1983): 26-32.

Elkind, David. "Helping Parents Make Healthy Educational Choices for Their Children." *Educational Leadership* 44 (November 1986): 36-39.

Eubanks, Eugene, and Parish, Ralph. "An Inside View of Change in Schools." *Phi Delta Kappan* 68 (April 1987): 610-15.

Feldman, Daniel C. "Diagnosing and Changing Group Norms." In *Developing Human Resources*. La Jolla, Calif.: University Associates, 1985.

Fisher, Norman. "James Madison High: A School for Winners." *American Education* 20 (November 1984): 10-15.

Frymier, Jack; Cornbleth, Catherine; Donmoyer, Robert; Gansneder, Bruce; Jeter, Jan; Klein, Frances; Schwab, Marian; and Alexander, William. *One Hundred Good Schools*. West Lafayette, Ind.: Kappa Delta Pi, 1984.

Fulbright, Luann. "Taking Charge of Your PR." *Here's How* 4 (June 1986). A two-page newsletter published by the National Association of Elementary School Principals, 1615 Duke Street, Alexandria, VA 22314.

Gallup, George H. "The 15th Annual Gallup Poll of the Public's Attitudes Toward the Public Schools." *Phi Delta Kappan* 65 (September 1983): 33-47.

Gargiulo, R.M., and Batson, J. "EPIC School: An Adventure in the Least Restrictive Alternative." *Education* 105 (1985): 394-95.

Glenn, Beverly C. "Excellence and Equity: Implications for Effective Schools." *Journal of Negro Education* 54 (1985): 289-301.

Glickman, Carl D. "Good and/or Effective Schools: What Do We Want?" *Phi Delta Kappan* 68 (April 1987): 622-24.

Goodlad, John I. *A Place Called School: Prospects for the Future.* New York: McGraw-Hill, 1983.

Gordon, Pamela, and Meadows, B.J. "Sharing a Principalship: When Two Heads Are Better Than One." *Principal* 65 (September 1986): 26-29.

Gotts, Edward E., and Purnell, Richard F. *Improving Home-School Communications.* Fastback 230. Bloomington, Ind.: Phi Delta Kappa Educational Foundation, 1985.

Gray, Sandra T. "How To Create A Successful School/Community Partnership." *Phi Delta Kappan* 65 (February 1984): 405-409.

Gray, William A. *Challenging the Gifted and Talented Through Mentor-Assisted Enrichment Projects.* Fastback 189. Bloomington, Ind.: Phi Delta Kappa Educational Foundation, 1983.

Greenleaf, Warren T. "A Turnaround Principal." *Principal* 63 (September 1983): 6-11.

Gregory, Thomas R., and Smith, Gerald R. *High Schools as Communities: The Small School Reconsidered.* Bloomington, Ind.: Phi Delta Kappa Educational Foundation, 1987.

Grossnickel, D. "Student Success Should Be More than a Cliche." *NASSP Bulletin* 70 (February 1986): 20-22.

Harbaugh, Mary. "Small Schools with Big Ideas." *Instructor and Teacher* 95 (September 1985): 138-40.

Hare, Isadora. "School Social Work and Effective Schools." *Urban Education* 22 (January 1988): 413-28.

Harrington, Theresa. "Annehurst School for Tomorrow." *Theory Into Practice* 13 (Spring 1974): 71-74.

Hantel, E.G. "Community Education and Implications for Leadership." *Tennessee Education* 13 (1983): 99-104.

Hodgkinson, Harold L. "The Right Schools for the Right Kids." *Educational Leadership* 45 (February 1988): 10-14.

Hodgkinson, Harold L. *All One System: Demographics of Education, Kindergarten Through Graduate School.* Washington, D.C.: Institute for Educational Leadership, 1985.

Holland, Kathleen. "The Impact of the Reading Recovery Program on Parents and Home Literacy Contexts." Doctoral dissertation, Ohio State University, 1987.

Holliday, A.E. "Put the Public Back into School P.R." *Updating School Board Policies* 11 (1980): 1-3, 5.

The Holmes Group. *Tomorrow's Teachers: A Report of the Holmes Group*. East Lansing, April 1986.

Howard, Eugene; Howell, Bruce; and Brainard, Edward. *Handbook for Conducting School Climate Improvement Projects*. Bloomington, Ind.: Phi Delta Kappa Educational Foundation, 1987.

Howe, Harold, II. "The Prospect for Children in the United States." *Phi Delta Kappan* 68 (November 1986): 191-96.

Hunter, Madeline. "Making Parents Collaborators." *Here's How* 4 (April 1986). A two-page newsletter published by the National Association of Elementary School Principals, 1615 Duke Street, Alexandria, VA 22314.

Hyder, L.R. "The Effectiveness of Communication Media Used in Tennessee Public School Systems." Doctoral dissertation, University of Tennessee, 1979.

Judge, Harry. *American Graduate Schools of Education: A View from Abroad*. New York: Ford Foundation, 1982.

Keesby, Forrest E. "Who Wrecked the Schools? Thirty Years of Criticism in Perspective." *Educational Theory* 34 (Summer 1984): 209-17.

Keller, Edward. "Put the CHOICE Act in Layaway — and Leave it There." *Communicator, Newsletter of the National Association of Elementary School Principals* 10 (October 1986): 7.

Kinder, J.A. *School Public Relations: Communicating to the Community*. Fastback 182. Bloomington, Ind.: Phi Delta Kappa Educational Foundation, 1982.

Kindred, L.W.; Bagin, Don; and Gallagher, E.G. *The School and Community Relations*. Englewood Cliffs, N.J.: Prentice-Hall, 1984.

Kirst, Michael W. "The Changing Balance in State and Local Power to Control Education." *Phi Delta Kappan* 66 (November 1984): 189-91.

Kirst, Michael W. "Loss of Support for Public Schools: Some Causes and Solutions." *Daedulus* 110 (Summer 1981): 45-68.

Kotler, Phillip. *Marketing for Non-Profit Organizations*. 2nd Ed. Englewood Cliffs, N.J.: Prentice-Hall, 1982.

Kyle, Regina M.J., and Allen, Edwin J., Jr. *Parental Choice of Education: A Literature Review of Significant Research*. Prepared for the School Finance Project of the National Institute of Education. Washington, D.C.: E.H. White, 25 January 1982.

Lane, John J., ed. *Marketing Techniques for School Districts*. Reston, Va.: Association of School Business Officials International, 1986.

Lapointe, Archie E., "The Good News About American Education." *Phi Delta Kappan* 65 (June 1984): 663-67.

Lasley, Thomas J., and Wayson, William W. "Characteristics of Schools with Good Discipline." *Educational Leadership* 40 (December 1982): 28-31.

Lasswell, Harold D. *A Preview of Political Science*. New York: American Elsevier, 1971.

Lathen, Calvin W., and Caudillo, Jess D. "Before You Agree to Share Facilities, Consider These Fourteen Crucial Issues." *American School Board Journal* 169 (June 1982): 30-31.

Lemmon, P. "A School Where Learning Styles Make a Difference." *Principal* 64 (March 1985): 26-28.

Levine, Daniel U.; Levine, Rayna F.; and Ornstein, Allan C. "Guidelines for Change and Innovation in the Secondary School Curriculum." *NASSP Bulletin* 69 (May 1985): 9-14.

Levine, A., and Haselkorn, D. "For the Sake of Children: The Demise of Educational Consensus in America." *National Forum* (Spring 1984): 5-10.

Lewis, Anne. "Affecting Disaffected Youths." *Phi Delta Kappan* 67 (April 1986): 555-56. *a*

Lewis, Anne. "Another Generation Lost?" *Phi Delta Kappan* 67 (March 1986): 483-84. *b*

Lewis, Anne. "Young and Poor in America." *Phi Delta Kappan* 67 (December 1985): 251-52. *a*

Lewis, Anne. "Bennett Uses 'Bully Pulpit' to Advance Ideological Agenda." *Phi Delta Kappan* 67 (September 1985): 3-4. *b*

Lightfoot, Sarah Lawrence. *The Good High School: Portraits of Character and Culture*. New York: Basic Books, 1983.

Lightfoot, Sarah Lawrence. "Portraits of Exemplary Secondary Schools." *Daedalus* 110 (1981): 17-38.

Lightfoot, Sarah Lawrence. *World's Apart: Relationships Between Families and School*. New York: Basic Books, 1978.

Lintz, M. Nan. "Do School-Community Relations Practices and/or Techniques Influence Confidence in the Public Schools?" *Mid-South Educational Researcher* 15 (December 1987): 9-18.

Lintz, M. Nan. "Practices and/or Techniques to Improve School-Community Relations and Develop Confidence in the Public Schools." Doctoral dissertation, University of Tennessee, 1987.

Lintz, M. Nan. "Attitudes of Teachers and Administrators Are a Key Influence in the Public's Confidence in Education." *Journal of Educational Public Relations* 8 (Summer 1985): 34-35.

Lintz, M. Nan. "Information and Communication: Tools for Increasing Confidence in the Schools." Paper presented at the American Educational Research Association Conference, April 1984. ERIC-RIE, ED 244-373

Lintz, M. Nan. "PR Tips: Use Community Involvement to Improve Public Relations." *Tennessee School Boards Journal* 4 (Spring 1984): 10-11.

Lipka, Richard P.; Beane, James A.; and O'Connell, Brian E. *Community Service Projects: Citizenship in Action.* Fastback 231. Bloomington, Ind.: Phi Delta Kappa Educational Foundation, 1985.

Lipset, Seymour M., and Schneider, W. "The Decline of Confidence in American Institutions." *Political Science Quarterly* 98 (Fall 1983): 379-402.

Lodish, Richard. "A School Alive." *Principal* 64 (January 1985): 28-31.

Long, Claudia. "How to Get Community Support." *Principal* 64 (May 1985): 28-30.

Lowe, Robert B., and Gervais, Robert L. "Tackling a Problem School." *Principal* 62 (May 1984): 8-12.

Mann, Des. *Correspondences: The Shaping of a School.* Palmerston North, New Zealand: Dunmore Press, 1987.

Manning, Alton C. *Adopt a School — Adopt a Business.* Fastback 263. Bloomington, Ind.: Phi Delta Kappa Educational Foundation, 1987.

McAuly, J. "Giving and Getting: A Study of Charitable Contributions." *School Business Affairs* 50, no. 2 (1984): 26-27, 41.

McCormick, Kathleen. "To Make Friends, Offer Adult Education." *American School Boards Journal* 169 (May 1982): 33-34.

McDonald, Alice. "Solving Educational Problems Through Partnerships." *Phi Delta Kappan* 67 (June 1986): 752-53.

McGreever, J.M. *The Origin of Ohio Households' Opinions About Public Education (Survey Report).* Charleston, W.Va.: Appalachia Educational Laboratory, October 1979.

McPherson, R. Bruce; Crowson, Robert L.; and Brieschke, Patricia A. "Marjorie Stallings: A Walk Through a Mine Field." *Urban Education* 21 (April 1986): 62-85.

McClurg, Richard C.; Ross, Daniel B.; and Ball, Richard A. "Letter to the Editor: Pickerington Schools." *Columbus Monthly* 13 (January 1987): 7.

McKee, Patricia; Wilson, Bruce L.; and Corcoran, Thomas B. "A Salute to Success: The Elementary School Recognition Program." *Principal* 66 (September 1986): 14-19.

McLaughlin, Milbray W.; Pfeifer, R. Scott; Swanson-Owens, Deborah; and Yee, Sylvia. "Why Teachers Won't Teach." *Phi Delta Kappan* 67 (February 1986): 420-26.

Marx, Gary. *Building Public Confidence in Our Schools.* Arlington, Va.: American Association of School Administrators, 1983.

Montana, Patrick J., ed. *Marketing in Nonprofit Organizations.* New York: American Management Associations, 1978.

Mott Foundation. *Community Education: Partnerships for Tomorrow.* Flint, Mich., 1982.

Murphy, Joseph F. "Effective Schools: What the Research Reveals." *APEX Case Report* 1 (February 1985). Available from APEX Center, 1310 S. Sixth Street, Champaign, IL 61820.

Murphy, Joseph F., and Hallinger, Philip. "Effective High Schools: What Are the Common Characteristics?" *NASSP Bulletin* 69 (January 1985): 18-22.

National Association of Elementary School Principals. "PR: An Education Priority." *Education Almanac.* Alexandria, Va.: NAESP, 1985.

National Coalition of Advocates for Students. *Barriers to Excellence: Our Children at Risk.* Boston, 1985.

National Commission on Excellence in Education. *A Nation at Risk: The Imperative for Educational Reform.* Washington, D.C.: U.S. Government Printing Office, 1983.

National Community Education Association. *Striving for Excellence with Community Education.* Washington, D.C., 1983.

National Education Association. *National Opinion Survey.* Washington, D.C., 1978.

National Governors' Association. *Time for Results: The Governors' 1991 Report on Education.* Washington, D.C., 1986.

National School Public Relations Association (NSPRA). *School Public Relations: The Complete Book. A Source Book of Proven PR Practices.* Arlington, Va., 1986.

National School Public Relations Association (NSPRA). *Shape of Education Kit for 1983.* Reston, Va., 1983. *Building Level School Communication Workshop Kit* also available.

Nathan, Joe. "Implications for Educators of *Time for Results.*" *Phi Delta Kappan* 68 (November 1986): 197-201.

Nathan, Joe. "The Rhetoric and the Reality of Expanding Educational Choices." *Phi Delta Kappan* 66 (March 1985): 476-81.

Neill, George. *The Local Education Foundation: A New Way to Raise Money for Schools.* Reston, Va.: National Association of Secondary School Principals, 1983.

Nolan, Fred, and Richardson, Marjorie. "Vistas Unlimited: A Success Story for Rural Principals." *Principal* 64 (March 1985): 34-36.

Norman, C.D. "A Study of Public Information Practices Among Selected School Systems of the United States." Doctoral dissertation, University of Tennessee, 1979.

Northwest Regional Laboratory. "School Improvement High Priority at Colville High." *Goal-Based Education* 37 (October 1984).

Novatis, Barbara. "How to Set Up a Realtors' Orientation." *The School Administrator* 42 (June 1985): 27-28.

Oakley, Hugh T. "Parental Choice of Elementary Schooling Alternatives in an Affluent Suburban Community." Doctoral dissertation, Ohio State University, 1985.

O'Connell, Carol. *How to Start a School/Business Partnership.* Fastback 226. Bloomington, Ind.: Phi Delta Kappa Educational Foundation, 1985.

Ornstein, Allan C. "Urban Demographics for the 1980's: Educational Implications." *Education and Urban Society* 16 (August 1984): 477-96.

Parkay, Forrest W. "A School/University Partnership That Fosters Inquiry-Oriented Staff Development." *Phi Delta Kappan* 67 (January 1986): 386-89.

Penick, John E.; Yager, Robert E.; and Bonstetter, Ronald. "Teachers Make Exemplary Programs." *Educational Leadership* 44 (October 1986): 14-20.

Peters, Thomas J., and Austin, Nancy. *A Passion for Excellence: The Leadership Difference.* New York: Random House, 1985.

Peters, Thomas J., and Waterman, R.H. *In Search of Excellence: Lessons from America's Best-Run Companies.* New York: Harper & Row, 1982.

Phi Delta Kappa Commission on Discipline. *Handbook for Developing Schools With Good Discipline.* Bloomington, Ind.: Phi Delta Kappa, 1982.

Pipho, Chris. "Student Choice: The Return of the Voucher." *Phi Delta Kappan* 66 (March 1985): 461-62.

Powell, Arthur G. "Being Unspecial in the Shopping Mall High School." *Phi Delta Kappan* 67 (December 1985): 255-61.

Rasinski, T.V. "Curricula for Caring: Overcoming the Alienation of the Young." *Humanistic Education and Development* 23 (1984): 88-95.

Ravitch, Diane. "A Good School." *American Scholar* 53 (1984): 481-93.

Raywid, Mary Ann, and Shaheen, J. "Diversity: Surviving and Thriving." *Early Years* 14 (May 1984): 28-31.

Robinson, Glen. *Effective Schools: A Summary of Research.* Alexandria, Va.: Educational Research Service, 1983.

Rossman, Gretchen B.; Corbett, H. Dickson; and Dawson, Judith A. "Intentions and Impacts: A Comparison of Sources of Influence on Local School Systems." *Urban Education* 21 (April 1986): 86-106.

Rowan, Brian; Bossert, Steven T.; and Dwyer, David C. "Research on Effective Schools: A Cautionary Note." *Educational Researcher* 12 (April 1983): 24-31.

Rury, John L. "Race and Common School Reform: The Strange Career of the NYSPECC, 1847-1860." *Urban Education* 20 (January 1986): 473-92.

Rutherford, William L. "School Principals as Effective Leaders." *Phi Delta Kappan* 67 (September 1985): 31-34.

Rutter, Michael. "School Influences on Children's Behavior and Development." *Pediatrics* 65 (February 1980): 208-20, 361.

Sarason, Seymour B. *The Creation of Settings and the Future Societies.* San Francisco: Jossey-Bass, 1972.

Sarason, Seymour B. *The Psychological Sense of Community: Prospects for a Community Psychology.* San Francisco: Jossey-Bass, 1974.

Sarason, Seymour. *Schooling in America: Scapegoat and Salvation.* New York: Free Press, 1983.

Schmitt, Donald. "Parents and Schools as Partners in Preschool Education." *Educational Leadership* 44 (November 1986): 40-41.

Schmuck, Richard A., and Runkel, Philip J. *The Handbook of Organization Development in Schools*. 3rd ed. Palo Alto, Calif.: Mayfield, 1985.

Scheier, Ronni. "Socrates Come to Austin." *Chicago* (June 1986): 128-30.

Seeley, David S. *Education Through Partnership: Mediating Structures and Education*. Cambridge, Mass.: Ballinger, 1980.

Seeley, David S. "Partnership's Time Has Come." *Educational Leadership* 44 (September 1986): 82-85.

Seeley, David S., guest editor. "Building Links Between Schools and Communities." *Phi Delta Kappan* 65 (February 1984). Entire Issue.

Sizer, Theodore R. *Horace's Compromise: The Dilemma of the American High School*. Boston: Houghton Mifflin, 1984.

Smith, Vernon, and Gallup, George. *What the People Think About Their Schools: Gallup's Findings*. Fastback 94. Bloomington, Ind.: Phi Delta Kappa Educational Foundation, 1977.

Sonnenfeld, David. *The Educational Marketplace: Toward a Theory of Family Choice in Schooling*. Eugene: University of Oregon Graduate School, May 1973.

Stedman, Lawrence C. "It's Time We Changed the Effective Schools Formula." *Phi Delta Kappan* 69 (November 1987): 215-24.

Stedman, Lawrence C. "A New Look at the Effective Schools Literature." *Urban Education* 20 (October 1985): 295-326.

Steers, Richard M. "Problems in the Measurement of Organizational Effectiveness." *Administrative Science Quarterly* 20 (1975): 546-58.

Stickney, John. "Why Schools Matter: Before You Buy a House, Do Your Homework First on Local Education." *Money* 15 (April 1986): 64.

Taylor, William D., and Johnson, Jane B. "Resisting Technological Momentum." In *Microcomputers and Educational Governance. Eighty-Fifth Yearbook of the National Society for the Study of Education*. Chicago: University of Chicago Press, 1986.

Thomas, Donald M., and Sorensen, LaVar. "South High School: An Effective Inner-City School." *NASSP Bulletin* 67 (November 1983): 36-39.

Tucker, Marc, and Mandel, David. "The Carnegie Report — A Call for Redesigning the Schools." *Phi Delta Kappan* 68 (September 1986): 24-27.

Vaill, Peter B. *The Practice of Organization Development*. Madison, Wis.: American Society for Training and Development, 1971.

Wayson, William W., and Lasley, Thomas J. "Climates for Excellence: Schools That Foster Self-Discipline." *Phi Delta Kappan* 65 (February 1984): 419-21.

Wayson, William W.; Mitchell, Brad; Pinnell, Gay Su, and Landis, David. *Up From Excellence: The Impact of the Excellence Movement on Schools*. Bloomington, Ind.: Phi Delta Kappa Educational Foundation, 1988.

Weiler, Hans H. "Education, Public Confidence, and the Legitimacy of the Modern State: Do We Have a Crisis?" *Phi Delta Kappan* 64 (September 1982): 9-14.

Weiler, Hans N. *Education, Public Confidence, and the Legitimacy of the Modern State: Is There a Crisis Somewhere?* Program Report no. 82-B4. Stanford, Conn.: Institute for Research on Educational Finance and Governance, June 1982.

West, Philip T. *Educational Public Relations.* Beverly Hills, Calif.: Sage, 1985.

West, Philip T. "To Sell or Not to Sell: Marketing in the Public Schools." *Catalyst for Change* 15 (Fall 1985): 15-17.

Wexler, Henrietta. "An Outstanding High School Breaks the Logjam of Mediocrity." *American Education* 20 (June 1984): 25-26.

Wherry, John H. "Restoring Confidence in the Schools." In *Marketing Techniques for School Districts*, edited by John J. Lane. Reston, Va.: Association of School Business Officials International, 1986.

Williams, Mary Frase; Hancher, Kimberly Small; and Hutner, Amy. "Parents and School Choice: A Household Survey." School Finance project working paper. Washington, D.C.: U.S. Department of Education, December 1983.

Wilson, Bruce L., and Rossman, Gretchen B. "Collaborative Links with the Community: Lessons from Exemplary Secondary Schools." *Phi Delta Kappan* 67 (June 1986): 708-11.

Wolf, Brent. "Turn Your Schools into Centers of Community Activity, and Win Broader Citizen Support." *American School Boards Journal* 169 (May 1982): 35.

Wolkimar, Richard. "The Winning Equation at 'P.S. IQ': Bright Kids, Good Teachers, Hard Work." *Smithsonian* 16 (May 1985): 80-88.

Young, Rufus; Leonard, J.; and Codianni, A. "The Change Process in Real Life: Tracking Implementation of Effective Schooling Elements in Project SHAL, St. Louis." Paper presented to the American Educational Research Association Conference, Montreal, 1983. ERIC No. ED 231 039

Young, Rufus; Leonard, J.; and High, Reginald. "Development and Use of a Replication and Evaluation Model to Track the Implementation of Effective Schools Elements in an Inner-City Setting (SHAL)." Paper presented to the Mid-South Educational Research Association annual meeting, 1984. ERIC No. ED 227 546, 015 440.

Appendix
Schools and Districts that
Contributed to the Study

This Appendix contains a list of the schools and districts that contributed to this study in a variety of ways. Most were nominated as
having high levels of confidence; and personnel from these school
districts returned questionnaires, which provided most of the data
we have reported. Others were described in the literature and were
included because they validated and corroborated the patterns observed in the nominated schools and districts. Still others, which did
not fall within the sample, were included because they had particular strengths that were highly prized by their communities and constituents.

Although these schools were selected because of their reputed high
public confidence, circumstances do change in American schools and
districts — sometimes quite rapidly. Consequently, they may not be
in 1988 what they were in 1984 and 1985 when we collected our
data. We cannot be sure that an observer will see the positive programs and practices reported in this book. However, we are sure
that one will find in these schools and districts people who have had
experience with programs and practices that are associated with improved achievement, self-disciplined staff and students, and high staff
morale, which earned them public confidence.

If they have survived policy changes that sometimes inhibit good
education and personnel changes that sometimes alter the character

of school boards, administration, and teaching staffs; if they have not succumbed to the easier rewards that come with cosmetic program changes; and if they have maintained their collegial commitment to problem solving and educating all children, they will continue to serve as models of institutions deserving of high public confidence.

Elementary Schools

A. C. Moore Elementary School
Columbia, South Carolina 29201

Aguilar Elementary School
Tempe, Arizona 85283

Alta S. Leary Elementary School
Warminster, Pennsylvania 18974

Annehurst Elementary School
Westerville, Ohio 43081

Arlington Elementary School
St. Louis, Missouri 63155

Bammel Elementary School
Houston, Texas 77090

Batavia Elementary School
Batavia, Ohio 45103

Bay Haven School of Basic Plus
Sarasota, Florida 33580

Beaver Run Elementary School
Salisbury, Maryland 21801

Blueberry Hill Elementary School
Longmeadow, Massachusetts 01106

Boones Creek Elementary School
Gray, Tennessee 37615

Boyd Elementary School
Omaha, Nebraska 68108

Brook Glenn Elementary School
Taylors, South Carolina 29687

Brook Park Memorial Elementary
  School
Brook Park, Ohio 44142

Burton Elementary School
Huntington Woods, Michigan 48070

Cascade Elementary School
Kennewick, Washington 99337

Cash Elementary School
Kernersville, North Carolina 27284

Centennial Elementary School
Broomfield, Colorado 80020

Chambers Elementary School
East Cleveland, Ohio 44112

Chapel Street School
Stratford, Connecticut 06497

Cheney Elementary School
Orlando, Florida 32807

Clemens Crossing Elementary
  School
Columbia, Maryland 21044

The College
Moultrie, Georgia 31768

Cooper/Weisberg Elementary School
Superior, Wisconsin 54880

Consolidated Elementary School
Kennebunkport, Maine 04046

Coronado Hills Elementary School
Denver, Colorado 80229

Crest Hill Elementary School
Casper, Wyoming 82601

Crossgates Elementary School
Toledo, Ohio 43614

Crownhill Elementary School
Bremerton, Washington 98312

Custer Elementary School
Monroe, Michigan 48161

Dean Road Elementary School
Auburn, Alabama 36830

Doctors Inlet Elementary School
Doctors Inlet, Florida 32030

Douglas Elementary School
Tyler, Texas 75702

Dove Anna McNabb Elementary
School
Paducah, Kentucky 42001

Edison Elementary School
Columbus, Ohio 43212

Emerson Elementary School
Tulsa, Oklahoma 74206

Emily Dickinson Elementary School
New York, New York 10025

Emma Morgan Elementary School
Paducah, Kentucky 42001

Ethel McKnight Elementary School
East Windsor, New Jersey 08520

Excelsior Elementary School
Excelsior, Minnesota 55331

Fanny Meyer Hillers Elementary
School
Hackensack, New Jersey 07601

Fisk-Howard Elementary School
New Orleans, Louisiana 70113

Florence Elementary School
Omaha, Nebraska 68112

Fort Washington Elementary School
Clovis, California 93613

Francis Scott Key Elementary
School
Arlington, Virginia 22201

Frank Porter Graham Elementary
School
Chapel HIll, North Carolina 27514

Franklin Park Elementary School
Fort Myers, Florida 33906

Franklin School
Newark, New Jersey 07102

Ganado Primary School
Ganado, Arizona 86505

Garrison Elementary School
New York, New York 10199

George E. Harris Elementary School
Las Vegas, Nevada 89121

Glendale Landmark Elementary
School
Glendale, Arizona 85301

Glenview Elementary School
Anaheim, California 92807

Green Run Elementary School
Virginia Beach, Virginia 23456

Hamilton Park Elementary School
Dallas, Texas 75243

Hardwick Elementary School
Hardwick, Vermont 05843

Leif Ericson Elementary School
Chicago, Illinois 60624

Lulu M. Ross Elementary School
Milford, Delaware 19963

Nathaniel Hawthorne Elementary
School
University City, Missouri 63130

Hayes Elementary School
Lakewood, Ohio 44107

Hempstead Elementary School
St. Louis, Missouri 63155

Hendricks Avenue Elementary School
Jacksonville, Florida 32207

Higginsport Elementary School
Higginsport, Ohio 45131

Holderness Central Elementary
School
Plymouth, New Hampshire 03264

Hudson Elementary School
Topeka, Kansas 66605

Kenneth E. Neubert Elementary
School
Algonquin, Illinois 60102

Kimball Elementary School
Seattle, Washington 98144

Kishwaukee Elementary School
Rockford, Illinois 61125

LaClede Elementary School
St. Louis, Missouri 63155

Linden Elementary School
Oak Ridge, Tennessee 37830

Lowell Elementary School
Watertown, Massachusetts 02172

Manaugh Elementary School
Cortez, Colorado 81321

Marshall Elementary School
Jackson, Mississippi 39212-2698

Meadowbrook Elementary School
Hillsdale, New Jersey 07642

Meadowlane Elementary School
Phenix City, Alabama 36867

Meadows Elementary School
Sugar Land, Texas 77478

Mesa Verde Elementary School
Tucson, Arizona 85726

Montezuma Creek Elementary
School
Montezuma Creek, Utah 84534

Neely Elementary School
Gilbert, Arizona 85234

Normandy Elementary School
Denver, Colorado 80202

North Casper Elementary School
Casper, Wyoming 82601

North East Elementary School
Kearney, Nebraska 68847

North Fayette Elementary School
Fayetteville, Georgia 30214

Northfield Elementary School
Gering, Nebraska 69341

North Loop Elementary School
El Paso, Texas 79915

Oak Park Elementary School
Tampa, Florida 33605

Oglethorpe Elementary School
Atlanta, Georgia 30314

Oxford School
Oxford, Connecticut 06483

Pershing Elementary School
University City, Missouri 63130

Phillips Elementary School
Pittsburgh, Pennsylvania 15203

Pinedale Elementary School
Rapid City, South Dakota 57702

Plymouth Elementary School
Plymouth, New Hampshire 03264

Pooler Elementary School
Pooler, Georgia 31322

P.S. 75 Elementary School
New York, New York 10025

Queen Mary Community School
North Vancouver, British Columbia

Ranch Heights Elementary School
Bartlesville, Oklahoma 74006

Reading Hilltop Community School
Reading, Ohio 45215

Roland Park Elementary School
Baltimore, Maryland 21210

Roosevelt Elementary School
Hutchinson, Kansas 67501

Roosevelt-Perry Elementary School
Louisville, Kentucky 40203

Root Elementary School
Fayetteville, Arkansas 72701

Roseland Elementary School
Mansfield, Ohio 44906

Ruth Moyer Elementary School
Fort Thomas, Kentucky 41075

Ryle Elementary School
Stamford, Connecticut 06904

Saint Stephens Indian School
Saint Stephens, Wyoming 82524

Sam Hughes Elementary School
Tucson, Arizona 85719

Scenic Hills Elementary School
Springfield, Pennsylvania 19064

Seagrove Elementary School
Seagrove, North Carolina 27341

Sears Elementary School
Kenai, Alaska 99611

Southport Elementary School
Southport, Indiana 46227

St. Anthony Park Elementary School
St. Paul, Minnesota 55108

Steele Elementary School
Mason, Michigan 48854

Stewart Primary School
Akron, Ohio 44307

Summit Drive Elementary School
Greenville, South Carolina 29609

Sunnyside Elementary School
Pullman, Washington 99163

Surratt Elementary School
Clint, Texas 79836

Tecumseh-Harrison Elementary
School
Vincennes, Indiana 47591

Thomas L. Marsalis Elementary
School
Dallas, Texas 75241

Tritt Elementary School
Marietta, Georgia 30062

Underwood Elementary School
Raleigh, North Carolina 27608

Way Elementary School
Bloomfield Hills, Michigan 48152

West Side Elementary School
Marietta, Georgia 30064

Westview Elementary School
Goose Creek, South Carolina 29445

William O. Schaefer Elementary
School
Tappan, New York 10983

Willyard Elementary School
Ravenna, Ohio 44266

Wilson Elementary School
Bellwood, Illinois 60104

Woodbury Elementary School
Woodbury, Minnesota 55125

York Elementary School
Medina, Ohio 44256

Yseleta Elementary School
El Paso, Texas 79910

Junior High/Middle Schools

Albion Junior High School
Strongsville, Ohio 44136

Annie Camp Middle School
Jonesboro, Arkansas 72401

Apache Junction Junior High School
Apache Junction, Arizona 85220

Appleseed Middle School
Mansfield, Ohio 44901

Arroyo Seco Junior High School
Valencia, California 91355

Auburn Middle School
Auburn, Maine 04210

Blevins Junior High School
Fort Collins, Colorado 80526

Bret Harte Intermediate School
Los Angeles, California 90052

Brookland Junior High School
Washington, D.C. 20017

Butler Middle School
Salt Lake City, Utah 84070

Calapooia Middle School
Albany, Oregon 97321

Carl Albert Junior High School
Midwest City, Oklahoma 73130

Carmody Junior High School
Lakewood, Colorado 80227

Cashmere Middle School
Cashmere, Washington 98815

Chastain Junior High School
Jackson, Mississippi 39206

Chinquapin Middle School
Baltimore, Maryland 21212

Cleveland Middle School
Detroit, Michigan 48233

Columbus Junior High School
Columbus, Nebraska 68601

Cromwell Middle School
Cromwell, Connecticut 06416

Davis County Middle School
Bloomfield, Iowa 52537

Desert-Hills Middle School
Kennewick, Washington 99337

Dixon Junior High School
Provo, Utah 84601

Douglas MacArthur Middle School
Jonesboro, Arkansas 72401

Drake Junior High School
Arvada, Colorado 80002

Duluth Middle School
Duluth, Georgia 30136

Eastview Middle School
Bath, Ohio 44210

Elizabethtown Area Middle School
Elizabethtown, Pennsylvania 17022

Fort Gratiot Intermediate School
North Street, Michigan 48049

Genoa Junior High School
Genoa, Ohio 43430

George Leyva Junior High School
San Jose, California 95122

Geyer Middle School
Fort Wayne, Indiana 46816

Hayes Junior High School
Youngstown, Ohio 44504

Hoover Middle School
Albuquerque, New Mexico 87111

Horace Mann Middle School
West Allis, Wisconsin 53214

Hugh Baine Junior High School
Cranston, Rhode Island 02910

Illing Junior High School
Manchester, Connecticut 06040

Indian Hills Junior High School
Des Moines, Iowa 50322

Jan Mann Opportunity North
Miami, Florida 33054

Jefferson Davis Junior High School
Jacksonville, Florida 32216

John C. Fremont Junior High School
Las Vegas, Nevada 89104

John D. Pierce Middle School
Grosse Pointe Park, Michigan 48230

John Ericsson Junior High School
Brooklyn, New York 11201

John J. Rhodes Junior High School
Mesa, Arizona 85202

John Muir Middle School
Wausau, Wisconsin 54401

Kearney Junior High School
Kearney, Nebraska 68847

Kenai Junior High School
Kenai, Alaska 99611

Keokuk Middle School
Keokuk, Iowa 52632

Kolb Junior High School
Rialto, California 92376

L.J. Schultz Middle School
Cape Girardeau, Missouri 63701

Lincoln Middle School
Pullman, Washington 99163

Louis Armstrong Middle School
Queens, New York 11369

Lounsberry Hollow Middle School
Vernon, New Jersey 07462

Lowe's Grove Junior High School
Durham, North Carolina 27713

Madison Middle School
St. Louis, Missouri 53139

Mason Middle School
Mason, Michigan 48854

Midview Middle School
Grafton, Ohio 44044

Milford Middle School
Milford, Delaware 19963

Mobridge Junior High School
Mobridge, South Dakota 57601

Moulton Middle School
Moulton, Alabama 35650

Perkins Middle School
Akron, Ohio 44313

Princeton Junior High School
Cincinnati, Ohio 45246

Raceland Junior High School
Raceland, Louisiana 70394

Raub Middle School
Allentown, Pennsylvania 18104

Rocky River Intermediate School
Rocky River, Ohio 44116

Robertsville Junior High School
Oak Ridge, Tennessee 37831-4999

Roehm Junior High School
Berea, Ohio 44017

Sacajawea Junior High School
Spokane, Washington 99203

Sherman Middle School
Mansfield, Ohio 44906

Soldotna Junior High School
Soldotna, Alaska 99669

Southern Nash Junior High School
Spring Hope, North Carolina 27882

Stowe Middle School
St. Louis, Missouri 63112

Taft Middle School
Albuquerque, New Mexico 87107

Terrace Hills Junior High School
Grand Terrace, California 92324

Theodore Roosevelt Gathings
   Intermediate School #158
Bronx, New York 10451

Toussaint L'Ouverture Middle
   School
St. Louis, Missouri 63104

Triadelphia Junior High School
Wheeling, West Virginia 26003

Van Hoosen Junior High School
Rochester, Michigan 48063

Venado Middle School
Irvine, California 92714

Vernal Middle School
Vernal, Utah 84078

Wasatch Middle School
Heber City, Utah 84032

West Junior High School
Colorado Springs, Colorado 80904

West Ottawa Middle School
Holland, Michigan 49423

Westchester Middle School
Chesterton, Indiana 46304

Wheeling Junior High School
Wheeling, West Virginia 26003

William H. Crocker Middle School
Hillsborough, California 94010

William H. Lemmel School
Baltimore, Maryland 21233

Woodrow Wilson Junior High
   School
Roanoke, Virginia 24018

Wooster Intermediate School
Stratford, Connecticut 06497

Senior High Schools

Air Academy High School
Colorado Springs, Colorado 80840

Alamogordo High School
Alamogordo, New Mexico 88310

Amelia High School
Amelia, Ohio 45102

Ames High School
Ames, Iowa 50010

Apollo High School
Owensboro, Kentucky 42301

Ardmore High School
Ardmore, Oklahoma 73401

Ashland High School
Ashland, Ohio 44805

Aurora High School
Aurora, Ohio 44202

Babylon High School
Babylon, New York 11702

Bartlesville High School
Bartlesville, Oklahoma 74003

Benjamin Franklin Senior High
   School
New Orleans, Louisiana 70118

Bloomington High School
Bloomington, Illinois 61701

Blue Springs High School
Blue Springs, Missouri 64015

Booker T. Washington Senior High
   School
Tulsa, Oklahoma 74106

Bountiful High School
Bountiful, Utah 84010

Brandon High School
Brandon, Florida 33511

Brandywine High School
Wilmington, Delaware 19803

Broad Ripple High School
Center for the Humanities
Indianapolis, Indiana 46206

Bronx High School of Science
Bronx, New York 10468

Brooklyn Tech High School
Brooklyn, New York 11217

Burlington County Vocational Tech
 School
Medford, New Jersey 08055

Butler High School
Vandalia, Ohio 45377

Callaway High School
Jackson, Mississippi 39206

Captain Shreve High School
Shreveport, Louisiana 71105

Cambridge Ridge and Latin High
 School
Cambridge, Massachusetts 02141

Camden High School
Camden, South Carolina 29020

Centennial High School
Ellicott City, Maryland 21043

Central High School
Cape Girardeau, Missouri 63701

Chandler High School
Chandler, Arizona 85224

Cheyenne Mountain High School
Colorado Springs, Colorado 80906

Clayton High School
Raleigh, North Carolina 27520

Clear Creek Secondary School
Idaho Springs, Colorado 80452

Cleveland High School
Portland, Oregon 97202

Clinton High School
Clinton, Illinois 61727

Clinton High School
Clinton, Mississippi 39056

Clovis West High School
Clovis, California 93612

Colville High School
Colville, Washington 99114

Comsewogue High School
Port Jefferson Station, New York
 11776

Crater High School
Central Point, Oregon 97502

Douglas S. Freeman High School
Richmond, Virginia 23229

Duluth High School
Duluth, Georgia 30136

Eagle Grove Community High
 School
Eagle Grove, Iowa 50533

Eastmoor High School
Columbus, Ohio 43216

Edmondson High School
Baltimore, Maryland 21229

Edwin R. Murrow High School
Brooklyn, New York 11230

Elizabethtown Area High School
Elizabethtown, Pennsylvania 17022

Ellington High School
Ellington, Connecticut 06029

Franklin High School
Reisterstown, Maryland 21136

Freer High School
Freer, Texas 78357

Grandview Heights High School
Columbus, Ohio 43212

Grosse Pointe South High School
Grosse Pointe, Michigan 48236

Hanover High School
Hanover, New Hampshire 03705

Havelock-Plover Community School
Havelock, Iowa 50546

Highland High School
Ft. Thomas, Kentucky 41075

Highland High School
Salt Lake, Utah 84106

Homewood-Flossmoor High School
Flossmoor, Illinois 60422

Independence High School
Independence, Kansas 67301

Irmo High School
Columbia, South Carolina 29210

James B. Conant High School
Hoffman Estates, Illinois 60194

Jefferson High School
Cedar Rapids, Iowa 52401

John Marshall High School
Oklahoma City, Oklahoma 73114

Katahdin High School
Sherman Station, Maine 04777

Kelly Walsh High School
Casper, Wyoming 82601

Kennebunk High School
Kennebunk, Maine 04043

Key West High School
Key West, Florida 33040

Kickapoo High School
Springfield, Missouri 65807

Lahser High School
Bloomfield Hills, Michigan 48013

Lake Park High School
Roselle, Illinois 60172

Lakewood High School
Lakewood, Ohio 44107

Lee County High School
Sanford, North Carolina 27330

Leonia High School
Leonia, New Jersey 07605

Libertyville High School
Libertyville, Illinois 60048

Lincoln High School
Portland, Oregon 97205

Liverpool High School
Liverpool, New York 13088

Lowell High School
San Francisco, California 94132

McComb High School
McComb, Mississippi 39648

Malabar High School
Mansfield, Ohio 44907

Manzano High School
Albuquerque, New Mexico 87112

Mt. Lebanon High School
Mt. Lebanon, Pennsylvania 15228

Norcross High School
Norcross, Georgia 30071

North Central High School
Indianapolis, Indiana 46206

Northern Valley Regional High
School
Demarest, New Jersey 07627

Oak Ridge High School
Oak Ridge, Tennessee 37830

Olympia High School
Olympia, Washington 98501

Parkway West Senior High
School
Ballwin, Missouri 63011

Pasco High School
Pasco, Washington 99301

Perry-Meridian High School
Indianapolis, Indiana 46217

Pine Bluffs High School
Pine Bluffs, Wyoming 82082

Pioneer High School
Yorkshire, New York 14173

Plantation High School
Plantation, Florida 33317

Pocomoke High School
Pocomoke City, Maryland 21851

Pontiac Central High School
Pontiac, Michigan 48056

Port Chester High School
Port Chester, New York 10573

Princeton High School
Cincinnati, Ohio 45246

Princeton High School
Princeton, West Virginia 24740

Quincy High School
Quincy, Massachusetts 02169

Ribault High School
Jacksonville, Florida 32203

Rockville High School
Rockville, Maryland 20850

Roscommon High School
Roscommon, Michigan 48653

Roy C. Ketcham High School
Wappingers Fall, New York 12590

San Jacinto High School
San Jacinto, California 92383

Shape American High School
APO, New York 09088

Soldotna High School
Soldotna, Alaska 99669

South Boston High School
Boston, Massachusetts 02205

South Kingston High School
Wakefield, Rhode Island 02880

South Eugene High School
Eugene, Oregon 97401

South High School
Salt Lake City, Utah 84115-1699

South Plantation High School
Plantation, Florida 33317

Southside High School
Fort Smith, Arkansas 72903

Spartanburg High School
Spartanburg, South Carolina 29302

Spring Valley High School
Columbia, South Carolina 29206

Strongsville High School
Strongsville, Ohio 44136

Sturgis High School
Sturgis, Michigan 49091

Stuyvesant High School
New York, New York 10003

Sunset High School
Beaverton, Oregon 97075

Teutopolis High School
Teutopolis, Illinois 62467

Thomas A. DeVilbiss High School
Toledo, Ohio 43613

Tilghman High School
Paducah, Kentucky 42001

Topeka West Senior High School
Topeka, Kansas 66604

Turpin Senior High School
Cincinnati, Ohio 45244

U-32 High School
Montpelier, Vermont 05602

Union High School
Hardwick, Vermont 05843

Union High School
Union, South Carolina 29379

Upper St. Clair High School
Upper St. Clair, Pennsylvania 15241

Varina High School
Richmond, Virginia 23231

Warren Central High School
Indianapolis, Indiana 46229

W.G. Enloe High School
Raleigh, North Carolina 27610

Whitehall Senior High School
Whitehall, Michigan 49461

Williamstown High School
Williamstown, Vermont 05679

Windsor-Forest High School
Savannah, Georgia 31499-6201

Winston Churchill High School
San Antonio, Texas 78216

Winter Park High School
Winter Park, Florida 32789

Woodson High School
Washington, D.C. 20066

Worthington High School
Worthington, Ohio 43085

Wyoming High School
Wyoming, Ohio 45215

Yorktown High School
Arlington, Virginia

School Districts

Academy School District #20
Colorado Springs, Colorado 80918

Akron City Schools
Akron, Ohio 44301

Albuquerque Public Schools
Albuquerque, New Mexico 87125

Apache Junction Unified School
   District
Apache Junction, Arizona 85220

Arlington Public Schools
Arlington, Virginia 22207

Austin Independent School District
Austin, Texas 78710

Bartlesville Public Schools
Bartlesville, Oklahoma 74003

Bayport-Blue Point #5
Bayport, New York 11705

Belle Fourche Schools
Belle Fourche, South Dakota 57717

Bellingham School District #501
Bellingham, Washington 98225

Bethleham Central School District
Delmar, New York 12054

Bloomfield Hills School District
Bloomfield Hills, Michigan 48013

Cape Girardeau Public Schools
Cape Girardeau, Missouri 63701

Cedar Rapids Community School
   District
Cedar Rapids, Iowa 52402

Charlotte-Mecklenberg Public
   Schools
Charlotte, North Carolina 28228

Chastain/Jackson Public Schools
Jackson, Mississippi 39206

Cherry Creek School District
Denver, Colorado 80202

Clayton School District
Clayton, Missouri 63105

Clovis Unified School District
Clovis, California 93612

Columbia Public School District
Columbia, Missouri 65201

District of Columbia Public Schools
Washington, D.C. 20004

Dunklin R-5
Herculaneum, Missouri 63048

Duval County Public Schools
Jacksonville, Florida 32216

East Cleveland City Schools
East Cleveland, Ohio 44112

East Lyme School District
East Lyme, Connecticut 06333

East York Board of Education
Toronto, Ontario

Elizabethtown Area School District
Elizabethtown, Pennsylvania 17022

Elyria City Schools
Elyria, Ohio 44035

Emporia Unified School District
#253
Emporia, Kansas 66801

Evansville-Vanderburgh School
Corporation
Evansville, Indiana 47708

Florence School District One
Florence, South Carolina 29501

Fort Thomas City Schools
Fort Thomas, Kentucky 41075

Fort Wayne Community Schools
Fort Wayne, Indiana 46802

Frontenac County Board of
Education
Kingston, Ontario

Galloway Township Public Schools
Smithville, New Jersey 08201

Glendale Elementary School District
Glendale, Arizona 85301

Greenhills-Forest Park Schools
Cincinnati, Ohio 45240

Grosse Point Public School System
Grosse Point, Michigan 48230

Gwinnett County Public Schools
Lawrenceville, Georgia 30245

High School District #128
Libertyville, Illinois 60048

Hilliard City School District
Hilliard, Ohio 43026

Howard County Public Schools
Ellicott City, Maryland 41043

Jackson Municipal Separate School
District
Jackson, Mississippi 39205

Kearney Public Schools
Kearney, Nebraska 68847

Kenai Peninsula Borough School
District
Soldotna, Alaska 99669

Kennewick School District No. 17
Kennewick, Washington 99336

Lake Washington School District
Kirkland, Washington 98033

Lakewood City Schools
Lakewood, Ohio 44107

Le Mars Community Schools
Le Mars, Iowa 51031

Lima City Schools
Lima, Ohio 45804

Lincolnwood Community School
District 74
Lincolnwood, Illinois 60645

Linden Community Schools
Linden, Michigan 48451

Macomb District #185
Macomb, Illinois 61455

Maine School Administrative
District #71
Kennebunk, Maine 04043

Mansfield City School District
Mansfield, Ohio 44901

Mason Public Schools
Mason, Michigan 48854

Mercer County Public Schools
Princeton, West Virginia 24740

Milford School District
Milford, Delaware 19963

Minnetonka School District #276
Excelsior, Minnesota 55331

Morris School District
Morris, New York 13808

Mt. Lebanon School District
Mt. Lebanon, Pennsylvania 15278

Mountain Brook City Schools
Mountain Brook, Alabama 35213

Mullan School District
Mullan, Idaho 83846

Natrona County School District #1
Casper, Wyoming 82601

North Vancouver Schools
North Vancouver, British Columbia

Oak Ridge Schools
Oak Ridge, Tennessee 37830

Oklahoma City Public Schools
Oklahoma City, Oklahoma 73106

Orleans Southwest Supervisory
   Union
Hardwick, Vermont 05843

Palatine Township High School
   District #211
Palatine, Illinois 60067

Pattonville Schools
St. Louis County, Missouri 63043

Penn-Harris-Madison School
   Corporation
Mishawaka, Indiana 46544

Perry Township Metropolitan
   School District
Indianapolis, Indiana 46227

Phoenixville Area School District
Phoenixville, Pennsylvania 19460

Pinellas County Schools
Clearwater, Florida 33516

Pittsburgh Public Schools
Pittsburgh, Pennsylvania 15219

Princeton City Schools
Cincinnati, Ohio 45234

Provo City Schools
Provo, Utah 84604

Pullman Public Schools
Pullman, Washington 99163

Quincy Public Schools
Quincy, Massachusetts 02169

Rapid City Area School District
Rapid City, South Dakota 57701

Ravenna City Schools
Ravenna, Ohio 44266

Region XIII ESC Schools
Austin, Texas 78752

Regional School District #13
Durham, Connecticut 06422

Roanoke City Public Schools
Roanoke, Virginia 24031

Rochester Public Schools
Rochester, Minnesota 55902

Roosevelt Public Schools
Roosevelt, New York 11575

Saint Cloud School District
Saint Cloud, Minnesota 56301

Salt Lake City Schools
Salt Lake City, Utah 84111

Savannah-Chatham County Public Schools
Savannah, Georgia 31401

School Administrative Unit #48
Plymouth, New Hampshire 03264

Shaker Heights City School District
Shaker Heights, Ohio 44120

Springfield Public Schools
Springfield, Missouri 65802

Stratford Public Schools
Stratford, Connecticut 06497

Superior School District
Superior, Wisconsin 54880

Tigard School District 23J
Tigard, Oregon 97223

Topeka Public Schools, U.S.D. 501
Topeka, Kansas 66611

Triad Community Unit District #2
St. Jacob, Illinois 62281

Tucson Unified School District
Tucson, Arizona 85719

Tupelo Municipal Separate School District
Tupelo, Mississippi 38802

Union Parish Schools
Farmerville, Louisiana 71241

Virginia Beach City Public Schools
Virginia Beach, Virginia 23456

Washington Township Metropolitan School District
Indianapolis, Indiana 46240

Williamsburg-James City County Schools
Williamsburg, Virginia 23187

Winnetka Public Schools
Winnetka, Illinois 60093

Zeeland Public Schools
Zeeland, Michigan 49464

Other Schools (Combined Grade Levels and Private)

Babylon Junior-Senior High School
Babylon, New York 11702

Bishop Foley High School
Madison Heights, Michigan 48071

Bishop Hendricken High School
Warwick, Rhode Island 02889

Briarcrest Baptist High School
Memphis, Tennessee 38119

Bridgewater Village School
Bridgewater, Vermont 05034

Brookside School
Waterville, Maine 04901

Cal Farley's Boys Ranch
Boys Ranch, Texas 79010

Charlotte Latin School
Charlotte, North Carolina 28207

Clara E. Coleman School
Glen Rock, New Jersey 07452

Clarence Sabbath School
River Rouge, Michigan 48218

Clear Creek Secondary School
Idaho Springs, Colorado 80452

Crowley's Ridge Academy
Paragould, Arkansas 72450

GE-RCA Development School
Bensalem, Pennsylvania 19020

George Mason Junior-Senior High School
Falls Church, Virginia 22043

Hanford Secondary School
Richland, Washington 99352

Havelock-Plover School
Havelock, Iowa 50546

Hazen Public High School
Hazen, North Dakota 58545

Hazen Union School
Hardwick, Vermont 05843

Highlands High School
Fort Thomas, Kentucky 41075

John Mullan Junior-Senior High
School
Mullan, Idaho 83846

Kadimah School of Buffalo
Buffalo, New York 14223

Mayo School
Chicago, Illinois 60653

Memphis State University Campus
Elementary School
Memphis, Tennessee 38152

Mt. Ararat School
Topsham, Maine 04086

Mt. Vernon Community School
Alexandria, Virginia 22305

New Garden Friends School
Greensboro, North Carolina 27420

Norwood-Norfolk Junior-Senior
High School
Norwood, New York 13668

Roland Park School
Baltimore, Maryland 21210

Saint Simon Stock Catholic School
Bronx, New York 10457

Sidwell Friends School
Washington, D.C. 20016

SHAL Program
St. Louis, Missouri 63155

St. Joseph School
Neola, Iowa 51559

Sudbury Valley School
Farmington, Maine 04938

Warner Christian Academy
South Daytona, Florida 32019

Woodland Hall Academy
Tallahassee, Florida 32308

DATE DUE			

Handbook 209632